Containing America

Cultural Production and Consumption in Fifties America

Edited by
Nathan Abrams and Julie Hughes

THE UNIVERSITY
OF BIRMINGHAM
UNIVERSITY PRESS

First published in the United Kingdom by The University of Birmingham Press, Edgbaston, Birmingham, B15 2TT, UK.

ISBN 0-902459-06-7

British Library Cataloguing in Publication data
A CIP catalogue record for this book is available from the British Library

Printed in Great Britain by

CONTENTS

INTRODUCTION

Nathan Abrams and Julie Hughes

The idea for this volume emerged from an interdisciplinary conference held at the University of Birmingham in November 1997, entitled *Containing Cultures: Complicity, Cooption, and Subversion in Fifties America.* A wide range of scholars from both Europe and America attended. We were impressed by this response, which indicated the range of current research and interest in new readings of 1950s Cold War production and consumption. Following the conference, we have since discovered that there is an even wider circle of scholars working in this field.

This collection represents a body of work building upon and extending the ground-breaking accounts of the 1950s by Lary May[1], Robert Corber[2] and Elaine Tyler May.[3] We hope to extend their work in new and original ways. Indeed, Alan Nadel's impressive *Containment Culture* provided the original stimulus for our thinking and theorising on 1950s culture with its linking of Cold War cultural and political narratives.[4] Between them, these works have covered a vast range of cinematic and literary output during the early Cold War period.

The essays in *Containing America* focus upon particular cultural products. The post-war period in America witnessed a tremendous consumer boom that introduced a whole range of new items into the mass market. As Emma Lambert points out, a plethora of cars, music systems, televisions and electrical appliances symbolised this emergent consumerism of the 1950s.

This influx of goods led to what Ben Andrews calls 'the expansion of everyday life'. This volume seeks to do justice to this expansion by amplifying the range of 1950s products that come under scholarly scrutiny. Rather than simply taking broad themes and genres, specific items were selected such as the theme park, the beauty shop, the radio, clothing, food, Batman comics, men's magazines, radioactivity in film, and popular fiction. Although some of these products have been examined before, most notably film, the new readings presented here will both complement and expand upon earlier studies by reflecting the most recent theoretical developments in the field. In this way, we hope that this volume will expand our conceptions of Cold War culture by focusing beyond non-cinematic and non-literary cultural production on such curiously neglected products as food and clothing.

We aim that *Containing America* will expand notions of production by examining a range of products outside the scope of previous studies. The choice of topics is by no means exclusive or all-encompassing. For example, popular music and performers such as Elvis are not included here, not least because studies of Elvis almost form a separate discipline in themselves. Nonetheless, we hope that this collection may serve as an indication of the many different ways to read cultural production and consumption during the height of the Cold War in America to both scholars and newcomers alike. What is more, these essays seek to explore everyday life, not merely its icons and outward surfaces. Clothes, food, magazines, radio and other forms of entertainment are examined in order to shed light on how Cold War discourses actually influenced the practices of ordinary behaviour. In this way, *Containing America* will point out directions for further research and provide a fresh approach for scholars, students and others interested in the culture of the Cold War of the 1950s.

This text also serves to widen our understanding of consumption by examining very different sectors of American society in terms of race, class and ethnicity in addition to sexuality and gender. Implicitly, notions of top-down cultural production will be challenged and expanded to include the processes of negotiation at all levels of American society. Consequently, *Containing America* emphasises the multiplicity, diversity and differing nature of the voices that emerged in cultural production and consumption during the Cold War of the 1950s. At the same time, however, common themes and similarities begin to emerge across the different sectors of American society. In particular, concerns about domesticity, masculinity, sexuality, technology, ethnicity, style and identity link these different voices of 1950s Cold War America. Overall, we hope to show the centrality of consumption to the processes of identity formation during this period and how consumer goods became important indices of status not least because, as Mark Jancovich observes, 'most Americans rate themselves against others through the ways in which they consume.'

By focusing on a range of 1950s products, we intend to show how dominant discourses such as those of containment, freedom, loyalty, radioactivity, masculinity, domesticity, sexuality, technology, conformity, consumption and America were produced, consumed and negotiated by varying sectors of American society. In doing so, we do not posit a monolithic culture of the 1950s. Rather, we hope to emphasise how the 1950s were, in the words of Bill Osgerby, 'a period of paradoxes, inconsistencies and contradictions', or as Mark Jancovich put it, the reconstruction of the 'complex social and cultural struggles that distinguish the period'. Cold War discourses did not function by means of a logical and rational set of propositions with an identifiable factual basis. They proceeded from a set of inconsistent, mutually contradictory concepts that could be deployed and redeployed at will. Indeed, the very active nature of consumption, adaptation and negotiation of the different sectors of US society heightened these inconsistencies, paradoxes and contradictions. As a result, the products that emerged were not unitary, and simply reflected hegemonic discourses passively and unproblematically.

The emphasis here, therefore, is very much on the nature of

active consumption and adaptation rather than passive reception. For example, Kyle Smith shows how in the context of the *Incredible Shrinking Man* (1957), ordinary consumer products such as pins, needles and thread were adapted and transformed into swords, grappling hooks and rope, rather than merely consumed. Julie Willett demonstrates how Cold War values were transfigured into the hairstyles of the 1950s. In this way, we hope to show that far from being a decade of passive conformity, the 1950s were an era of activity, what W.T. Lhamon has called 'deliberate speed'.[5] While some texts have dealt with similar aspects of the 1950s, they have done so as if culture existed within a political vacuum. The most recent example of this is the collection edited by Joel Foreman, *The Other Fifties: Interrogating Midcentury American Icons*.[6] A definitive history of the Cold War or the 1950s will not be produced here. It will be assumed that readers will come to this text with some understanding of the events that formed the backdrop to the topics discussed in this volume.

It is premised in *Containing America* that the Cold War and the 1950s were linked inextricably, that the former provided the immediate context to the latter, and that the Cold War provided an extremely fertile context for vigorous cultural production. The defining cultural moment and the genesis of the Cold War was the Truman Doctrine (delivered 12 March 1947). The speech established a set of universal structural categories or discourses through which the world was subsequently to be defined and understood. A series of speeches, initiatives and documents later expanded Truman's original categories into a set of complex yet interrelated discourses. Together, these speeches, initiatives, and documents privileged certain discourses. In particular, notions of freedom, individualism, loyalty, America and, of course, containment began to emerge. These discourses soon became the dominant cultural capital that was filtered throughout all sections of American society during the Cold War.[7]

This book has been arranged so that each chapter will build upon and complement its predecessor. The opening chapters by

Mark Jancovich and Emma Lambert both provide useful cultural contextualisation for those that follow. Jancovich analyses the discourses of conformity and their deployment by different sections of society. By examining the intellectuals, new middle classes, new white-collar workers, and Cold War experts, Jancovich argues that 'the discourse of conformity was central to the cultural politics of the period.' He states that almost every section of society sought to dissociate itself from conformity and to associate the term with those sections from which they wanted to distance themselves. In the course of his discussion, Jancovich highlights how personality and the self became commodified products to be bought and sold during the 1950s. In this way, identity was linked inextricably to consumption practices; for example, he notes the 'status panic' of the white-collar worker: the desperate need to define oneself through consumption and status symbols.

In contrast, Lambert focuses upon the opening of Disneyland in Anaheim, California in 1955. Despite a profusion of Disney scholarship, no writer to date has examined properly the relationship between the park and the cultural and political environment of the Cold War in which it was created. By reading the park itself and elements of its internal narratives, Lambert examines the productivity of the park in terms of the creation, consumption and negotiation of national identity during the early Cold War. In doing so, she illustrates not only the production of meanings within the park, but also the extent to which the park became an unofficial 'ambassador' to the rest of the world, taking its place as a national monument alongside those on the Mall in Washington, DC.

Willett demonstrates how 'beauty shop culture – everything from the conversations to the coiffures' in both Euro- and African-American communities simultaneously reinforced and undermined the dominant Cold War discourse of containment that dictated that women and the domestic were synonymous. Rather than simply mirroring the codes of containment, Willett argues that 1950s hairstyles helped both white and black women to challenge the politics of containment. Furthermore, she concludes that beauty shops were important sites of resistance enabling women to renegotiate their familial roles and their contributions to the family economy and to their communities. Willett's chapter provides an important ethnic and racial dimension to this volume and expands the locations of cultural production and consumption beyond white, mainstream areas.

The emphasis on non-cinematic forms of consumption, production and resistance is extended in Candida Taylor's chapter. Like Willett, she examines another form of style. Taylor takes as her text the zoot suit – the style innovated by the *pachucos*, the Hispanic dandies that emerged on the streets of Los Angeles in the final years of World War II. Taking Dick Hebdige's observation that style is a form of 'intentional communication', she focuses upon the appropriation of the zoot suit during the 1950s as an example of white youth rebellion against the dominant codes of containment and conformity. Following the example set by Elvis, by wearing the suit, whether intentionally or not, white youths located themselves within a tradition of dissent and criminal behaviour that originated during World War II. Consequently, these white youths took on for themselves a style of 'un-Americanism'. While the zoot suit was not 'produced' during the 1950s, it was actively adapted and incorporated into a style that self-consciously projected a resistance to the culture of containment, what was perceived to be the stultifying boredom of middle-class suburbia.

Continuing the focus on ethnic communities, Nathan Abrams examines the American-Jewish community of the 1950s. In particular, he studies the role and meanings of another neglected 1950s product, food. While 1950s food has been studied, the topic of ethnic food strangely marks an absence in our understanding of 1950s culture. Taking the key piece of evidence in the conviction of the Rosenbergs for atomic espionage – a box of Jell-O – he argues that non-kosher foods came to symbolise un-Americanism while traditional and kosher food products signified loyalty. Consequently, new mass-produced Jewish food products such as

Mother's Old-Fashioned Gefilte Fish were marketed as being traditional yet American. In this way, Jewish Americans invested their food products with contextual political meanings that assisted their mobility into the mainstream on their own terms. As such, Abrams demonstrates how dominant Cold War discourses penetrated to the very heart of everyday existence.

Ben Andrews adopts a cultural studies approach to examine the popular material culture of radio. In particular, he looks at John Cage and his concern for how listening had become seemingly effortless and music pre-packaged in post-war America as 'Aunt Jemima's ready-mix pancakes extended to the field of music'. John Cage's work in the 1950s provides an insight into the dissemination of broadcast sound, thus linking the concerns of Cold War scholarship, the domestic technology of 'everyday life' and the cosmic technology of 'outer space'. Radio was already a feature of household life by the 1950s, but the number of sets produced expanded massively during this period, as did its use in the propaganda war against the Soviet Union. Short-wave broadcasts had been controlled during the Korean War and the incorporation of short wave into his compositions almost implicated Cage within the coded messages of Cold war espionage. At the same time, Cage also seemed to express a similarity with the overt Cold War discourse of freedom. Implementing a revised musicology, Cage established new musical creations through a specific mode of listening and sought to liberate music from the confines of harmony and tonal cliché. Through his use of the radio in his compositions, Cage attempted to prevent the death of 'simply listening' by spreading music away from the concert hall into the lounges of America as the site for the consumption and reception of music. Since the advent and growth of television, the hearth and the radio as the central spaces in the American home had been superseded.

Like Andrews' chapter, Kyle Smith's chapter also addresses the extension of cosmic technology into every day life. Taking the film *The Incredible Shrinking Man* (1957) as his case study, Smith highlights an important backdrop to the decade of the 1950s:

radiation. He explains how Cold War fears of atomic and hydrogen technology were refracted through the insertion of radiation into science fiction movies of the 1950s as a convenient plot and marketing device. He juxtaposes filmic fictions with medical realities, whereby many patients were injected with radioactive materials as part of the ongoing experimentation with nuclear technology during the Cold War. Radiation for Smith thus becomes another product aimed at a particular teenage market, but even more exclusive since it could not be purchased as easily as radios, televisions, food and clothing. He then goes on to show how radiation and the bomb were linked to the domestic, so as to make it a more ordinary, everyday product. Smith's chapter helps to flesh out Cold War movie production beyond a narrow focus on B-movies and fantasies of alien invasion.

Taken together, Andrews and Smith point to the two sides of the consumer technology during the Cold War. On the one hand, the new gadgets of the consumer-driven 1950s culture such as radio and television were a positive force in many Americans' lives as forms of leisure and entertainment. On the other hand, this new technology, particularly in the form of atomic and nuclear power, had a destructive potential, fears of which were refracted through films such as *The Incredible Shrinking Man*. Paradoxically, therefore, 1950s Cold War culture simultaneously exhibited a fascination with technology as well as a phobia of it.

Bill Osgerby examines one of the more curious, but rarely acknowledged, publishing phenomena of the 1950s. Beginning in the late 1940s, there appeared a new wave of 'men's true adventure magazine's and 'macho pulps', with titles such as *Real* and *Saga*. These magazines revived many of the stylistic codes of their 1920s and 1930s predecessors, while simultaneously embodying the specific preoccupations and anxieties of the 1950s. In doing so, they constructed what Osgerby calls 'a masculine universe that combined a swaggering and misogynistic brutality with a profound set of social and sexual anxieties'. The eagerness of these magazines to assert a ruggedly virile masculinity, combined with an obsession with sexual violence, sadism and the testing of manhood, reaffirmed the Cold War discourse of domestic and sexual containment. Thus, they targeted women as a threat to traditional masculine identities, which, in turn, were over-exaggerated as a form of compensation. But while these magazines initially reflected the dominant discourse of containment, by the mid-1950s a discourse of conspicuous consumption became more prominent. The rough-and-ready world of the 'action man' was supplanted by the 'playboy' and his quest for personal gratification in a hedonistic, swinging world of endless leisure, luxury and lascivious indulgence. This new world was reflected *par excellence* in *Playboy* magazine, launched in 1953.

But while the more obvious Cold War discourses of domestic and sexual containment may have declined in these magazines, they were merely replaced by another discourse that was none the less actively encouraged in this period. As Lambert points out in her chapter on Disneyland, the freedom to consume was linked closely to the political discourses of the Cold War and was one of the main propaganda weapons used against the Soviet Union. Thus, conspicuous consumption represented a particularly Cold War form of activity.

Will Brooker focuses upon 1950s comics, in particular Batman and Robin. In doing so, he defends Dr Frederic Wertham's accusation in the 1950s that Batman and Robin represent 'a wish-dream of two homosexuals living together'. He argues that Wertham's critique makes visible and brings to light a level of homoerotic meaning at a time when homosexuality was demonised within America. Following the Federal Employee Loyalty Program of 1947, government persecution of homosexuals in federal employment increased in direct proportion to the intensification of the Cold War. Brooker's reading of Batman suggests that the comics projected a 'variety of subtle clues' that portrayed the very real difficulties of being a homosexual during the Cold War of the 1950s. In doing so, Brooker extends the very interesting work begun by Corber and D'Emilio beyond purely literary and cinematic forms of entertainment.

The popular best-selling fiction written by women during the 1950s has received limited critical attention from literary historiography. When considered at all, it is generally assumed that as a cultural form it reflected the containment and gender constraints of the decade, such as those depicted by Elaine Tyler May. Seeking to address this unbalanced view, Julie Hughes analyses Anya Seton's best-selling novel, *The Winthrop Woman* (1958). Hughes overcomes concepts that deny any form of contradiction or female agency in these novels. Instead, she shows how the production and consumption of best-selling fiction written by women for women may be read as a cultural barometer of discourses of discontent during the 1950s. Deploying a close textual reading of *The Winthrop Woman*, Hughes argues that Seton problematises the categories of history, fiction and biography. As such, she claims that Seton's historical romance may be read not only as a critique of the pursuit of 'objective' historical truth in the historical profession of the 1950s, but also as a rewriting of the history of America itself. Focusing upon the links between the America past and Cold War national identity, Hughes compares Seton to the emerging discipline of American studies that Christopher Lasch has called a propagandist exercise of the Cold War. While the overwhelming ideological pluralism sought to contain dissonance in American history by emphasising what had united Americans rather than what had divided them, Seton introduced ambiguity into the study of Puritanism during the Cold War. In this way, Hughes claims that Seton placed the 'invisible woman' at the centre rather than the margins of Cold War history.

Notes

1. Lary May, *Recasting America: Culture and Politics in the Age of Cold War* (Chicago, University of Chicago Press, 1989).
2. Robert Corber, *In the Name of National Security: Hitchcock, Homophobia, and the Political Construction of Gender in Postwar America* (Durham and London, Duke University Press, 1993) and *Homosexuality in Cold War America: Resistance and the Crisis of Masculinity* (Durham and London, Duke University Press, 1997).

3. Elaine Tyler May, *Homeward Bound: American Families in the Cold War Era* (New York, Basic Books, 1988).
4. Alan Nadel, *Containment Culture: American Narratives, Postmodernism, and the Atomic Age* (Durham and London, Duke University Press, 1995).
5. W.T. Lhamon, *Deliberate Speed: The Origins of a Cultural Style in the American 1950s* (Washington and London, Smithsonian Institution Press, 1990).
6. Joel Foreman, *The Other Fifties: Interrogating Midcentury American Icons* (Urbana and Chicago, University of Illinois Press, 1997).
7. For more detail on this process and these discourses, see Nathan Abrams, 'Struggling for Freedom: Arthur Miller, the *Commentary* Community, and the Cultural Cold War', (unpublished Ph.D. dissertation, University of Birmingham, 1998), especially Chapter 4.
8. Lynn Boyd Hinds and Theodore Otto Windt, *The Cold War as Rhetoric: The Beginnings, 1945–1950* (New York, Prager, 1991).

CHAPTER ONE

Othering conformity in post-war America: intellectuals, the new middle classes and the problem of cultural distinctions

Mark Jancovich

Representations of 1950s Cold War America are often simplistic and rarely give a sense of the period's complex and contradictory character. Part of the problem is that the identity of this period has frequently been constructed precisely as a simplistic, homogeneous and conformist one, against which latter periods can be defined as either a liberation or a fall. As a result, the period is presented as one of morality or repression, of harmony or complacency, of consensus or conformity.

Popular memory has been able to sustain contradictory images of the period, so that it has become a period of *both* complacency *and* paranoia, a period remembered for its mindless conformity *and* for its numerous figures of non-conformity and dissent. Indeed, so prevalent were the figures of heroic non-conformity during the 1950s that, as Barbara Klinger has claimed, it is Rock Hudson, a star whose image represented 'a wholesome, conventional, ultra-American, and pristine masculine type' who can be seen as an '"alternative" masculine ideal' when compared with the 'brooding, introspective portraits of masculinity' represented by stars such as Brando and Dean.[1]

These non-conformists are, of course, seen as rebelling against an amorphous, conformist Other, but, as Daniel Bell argued at the time, 'The curious fact, perhaps, is that no one in the United States defends conformity. Everyone is against it, and probably everyone always was.'[2] If there was one thing to which all Americans seemed to subscribe during the post-war period, it was that conformity was a bad and dangerous thing.

If we are to make sense of the period, we need to move beyond the opposition between the conformist and the non-conformist. It is not simply that, as Bell argues, almost everyone in the period seemed to see conformity as the enemy, but that they did so because the discourse of conformity was central to the cultural politics of the period. Indeed, the repeated attacks on conformity should not be seen as evidence of simplicity, homogeneity, conformity or political apathy. On the contrary, an analysis of its deployment by different sections of society can enable the reconstruction of the complex social and cultural struggles that distinguish the period.

Indeed, almost every section of society sought to disassociate itself from conformity and to associate the term with those sections from which they wanted to distance themselves. In politics, for example, both left and right associated each another with conformity. Some presented the suburban family as a bulwark against conformity, while others presented this institution as the epitome of conformity within the period. The conformist was always the degraded Other, a figure whose inferior status could be used to confirm the superiority of the autonomous, individual self. Unthinking conformity was how *other* people behaved. In short, the debates over conformity were part of the fierce and complex battles for distinction and authority that distinguished the period.

For example, the Cold War liberalism that distinguished the 1950s should be seen as an extremely complex discourse in which consensus was not, as is often argued, synonymous with a repression of dissent and a celebration of conformity. On the contrary, it required a very careful and precarious balancing act between the stimulation of difference, diversity and non-conformity *and* its containment. America was not presented as a society that had overcome all its problems, but rather as a society whose superiority to totalitarianism lay precisely in its encouragement of dissent and in its consequent ability to acknowledge, and thus tackle, its problems. In this framework, then, conformity was associated directly with the foreign, totalitarian Other, and nothing was more quintessentially American than the heroic dissenter, of which Martin Luther King would come to be seen as the exemplar by the late 1950s and early 1960s.

However, Cold War liberals did not suggest, as Andrew Ross claims, that totalitarianism was so foreign to American society that it 'couldn't happen here'.[3] The figures that Ross lists may have favoured a pluralist model of American politics, and even have seen totalitarianism as a foreign Other. Nonetheless, they were haunted by that Other, and by the difficulty of establishing the line that distinguished it from the liberal American self.

As a result, the preservation of liberty required eternal vigilance to prevent not only the Other from subverting the system, but also a descent into complacency in which the liberal self would become no different from the totalitarian Other. The most common internal threat for these critics was that of capitalism itself, a force that many saw as threatening to undermine liberalism and establish totalitarianism within America. According to Arthur M. Schlesinger Jr, for example, it represented two dangers: 'Capitalism, in brief, at once strengthens the economic centralization and loosens the moral bonds of society.'[4] The first of these problems was of most immediate concern to American post-war liberals, who produced a long-running debate on the problems of rationalisation and bureaucratisation.[5] The second problem, however, gained increasing significance from the end of the decade to the present and has been variously referred to as 'the cultural contradictions of capitalism', 'the culture of narcissism' and 'the crisis of legitimation'.[6]

INTELLECTUALS, CONFORMITY AND THE NEW MIDDLE CLASSES

Both criticisms, however, were connected intimately to a more general preoccupation with the middle class, or more specifically, a section of the middle class that has been variously termed 'the new class',[7] 'the professional-managerial class',[8] and 'the new petite bourgeoisie'.[9] This class has a problematic status for Cold War critics, for whom it was both the major social problem of the period and the primary solution. At times, the class was presented as a solution to social problems, as a class that offered the possibility of a society administered by a rational technocracy rather than by a political ideology. But at other times it was seen as the epitome of mediocrity, a mediocrity that made it not a bulwark against totalitarianism but provided the perfect conditions for its development.

For example, while Cold War critics such as Schlesinger identified totalitarianism as a system that gave individuals a sense of belonging and relieved them of the responsibility of making decisions for themselves,[10] it was exactly these features that William Whyte associated with the culture of 'the organization man'. While Whyte is careful to emphasise that he is not simply calling for non-conformity, he does present the organisation man as one 'who most urgently wants to belong'.[11] Indeed, Whyte plays with the term 'belonging' throughout his study. For example, while he argues that the organisation men are those who want to belong, he also claims that they are not simply those who 'only work for The Organization', but those who '*belong* to it as well'.[12] Belonging is not simply about feeling that one is part of something, but also implies that one is possessed by it. Belonging is therefore equivalent to slavery and even demonic possession: according to Whyte, the organisation does not just want your work, it 'wants your soul'.[13]

According to Whyte, then, the 'bureaucratization of society'[14] led to a situation in which individuals had over-learnt the values of co-operation and could no longer dissent from the group. This problem is associated with two main causes: on the one hand, the organisation had become so benevolent that individuals over-valued it and over-identified themselves with it; but on the other, their practices within the organisation had trained them too well. As Whyte puts it, 'Organization life being what it is, out of sheer necessity [the organisation man] must spend most of his working hours in one group or another, and out of self-defence, if not instinct, the committee arts must become a reflex to him.'[15]

This situation becomes a danger not only to the individual, but also to society. For Whyte, the over-valuation of co-operation was a threat to the health of both the organisation and American society as a whole. Co-operation may be necessary for the administration of systems once they have been instituted but 'not for creating them'. As a result, Whyte argues that to focus 'on agreement is to intensify that which inhibits creativity'.[16] If American corporations are to flourish and the American economy is to remain competitive, the organisation man has to learn how to disagree as well as how to co-operate. He has to learn to question, to challenge and to provoke others. Co-operation may be necessary to society but not at the expense of diversity and dissent.

If, however, Whyte saw the organisation man as lacking in creativity, C. Wright Mills argued that it was the nature of his work that was responsible because it provided little or no room for creativity. Rather than a new class of technocrats with decision-making powers, Mills presents the new white-collar workers as little more than a proletarianised middle class. These new white-collar workers had become merely 'interchangeable parts of the big chains of authority that bind society together'.[17] Their work requires nothing from them as individuals, and forces them to shed their individuality so that, as individual workers, they become indistinguishable to one another. They are compelled to conform to the demands of the organisation as a whole and their function within it in particular.

In this way, they are condemned to a position in which they not only lack control over the work process, but are also doomed to keep 'going year after year through the same paper routine'.[18] However, if the blue-collar worker suffers a similar form of 'alienated labour', in the case of the white-collar worker, 'the alienation of the wage-worker from the products of his work is carried one step nearer to its Kafka-like completion. The salaried employee does not make anything'.[19] Even then, however, the alienations of this class are not at an end. These workers do not work *on things*, but *with people* and, as a result, they become alienated even from their own personalities and feelings: 'When white-collar people get jobs, they sell not only their time and energy but also their personalities. They sell by the week or month their smiles and their kindly gestures, and they must practise the prompt repression of resentment and aggression.'[20]

The self is no longer a private and personal form of inalienable property, but becomes a commodity to be sold on 'the personality markets [where] emotions become ceremonial gestures by which status is claimed, alienated from the inner feelings they supposedly express.'[21]

CONFORMITY, CONSUMPTION AND THE NEW MIDDLE CLASSES

If personalities could be sold, they could also be bought, and it became common for commentators to claim that identity was no longer associated with production but rather with consumption. One of the major concerns about the new white-collar worker was therefore their supposed 'status panic': their desperate need to define themselves through their consumption practices. For some, like Whyte, this 'status panic' was seen as a desire to keep up with the neighbours, to blend in and avoid standing out as different from others. For others, such as Mills and Packard, it was seen as the desire to establish difference and distinction. In this second instance, 'status panic' is seen as an attempt to establish one's superiority to others through one's consumption practices and so, hopefully, to become more socially mobile.

Indeed, for Packard, it is in this area that class differences become most clear and pronounced. While many commentators claimed that the period was distinguished by the erosion or even disappearance of class, Packard argued that, on the contrary, 'Class lines in several areas of our national life appear to be hardening.'[22] For Packard, while 'the boundary between white-collar and blue-collar is blurring, the boundary between lower and upper white-collar groups is becoming sharp and formidable.'[23] Rather than a classless society, Packard therefore presents post-war America as a deeply divided class society, one in which there is a deep competition for advancement within the lower white-collar classes.

However, as Packard argues, one of the major markers of class are one's consumption practices, and most Americans rate themselves against others through the ways in which they consume. As Packard puts it, most Americans 'believe that some people rate somewhere above them, that some others rate somewhere below them, and that still others seem to rate close enough to their own level to permit them to explore the possibility of getting to know them socially without fear of being snubbed or appearing to downgrade themselves.'[24] However, this process of rating oneself and others is tied largely to the forms of consumption that distinguish specific classes, so that 'most of us surround ourselves, wittingly or unwittingly, with status symbols we hope will influence the raters appraising us, and which we hope will help establish some social distance between ourselves and those we consider below us.'[25]

Consumer skill therefore becomes essential not only to maintaining one's social standing but also to the achievement of social mobility. However, Packard argues, for this very reason, those 'less expert in the nuances of status symbols or more indifferent to them persist in modes of behaviour and in displays of taste that themselves serve as barriers in separating us from the group to which we may secretly aspire.'[26] These symbols of status are therefore not only the cars one drives and the home in which one lives, but also the clothes one wears, the food one eats and the alcohol one drinks. All of these modes of consumption signify one's self, identity and social position, whether intended or not.

It is in this context that Packard attacks the advertisers and particularly the 'motivation researchers'. For Packard, most advertising works beneath the level of consciousness and seeks to address and even stimulate subconscious anxieties, so that the act of consuming a particular product can be offered as a solution to those anxieties. Indeed, Packard argues that much advertising presents consumer goods as 'projections' of the consumer's self, so that it is not so much objects that are sold but 'self-images'.[27] Packard's complaint is that such techniques not only manipulate but also increasingly involve a subconscious mind-management in which the privacy of the individual consciousness and identity is under threat. As he argues, 'The most serious offence many of the depth manipulators commit, it seems to me, is that they try to invade the privacy of our minds. It is this right to privacy in our minds – privacy to be either rational or irrational – that I believe we must strive to protect.[28]

Advertising threatens the distinction between self and other on which the notion of individual identity depends, and it encourages individuals to conform unconsciously to the marketing strategies of the markers of consumer goods.

EXPERTS, THE MEDIA AND THE PROBLEM OF CULTURAL AUTHORITY

In this sense, Packard's argument bears similarities to a whole series of other critics for whom the human experience was increasingly mediated or managed by experts so that a 'thicket of unreality ... stands between us and the facts of life.'[29] As Daniel Boorstin claims, for example, the world of experience is increasingly dominated by 'the image' in which we have lost touch with 'reality' and encounter 'the increasing secondhandness of experience'.[30] He may claim to be 'unimpressed' by the 'villainy' of 'the hidden persuaders, the organisation men, Madison Avenue, Washington bureaucracy, the eggheads, the anti-intellectuals, the power elite, etc.'[31] but he nonetheless blames this loss of the real on the intervention of experts. These experts, he claims, not only mediate between people and reality but in the process tell them what to think and how to behave. He therefore castigates the editors of the *Reader's Digest* for predigesting works for its readers. Indeed, Boorstin even carefully and ironically positions his own volume in opposition to the numerous self-help books of the 1950s, and argues: 'This is a "how-not-to-do-it" book.'[32]

Thus, while historians such as Elaine Tyler May have claimed that the 1950s witnessed 'the near deification of the post-war professional',[33] this period actually displayed a deep ambivalence about experts. On the one hand, they were seen as threatening to introduce the very conformist behaviour associated with totalitarianism, in which the individual is relieved of the anxiety of choice and told how to act. On the other hand, they were seen as offering the new white-collar workers, who suffered from profound status anxiety, the very lifestyle guides that their situations demanded.

None the less it was precisely this relationship of the new white-collar workers to experts that was demonised by the post-war intellectuals. For example, Mills presented this new class as an essentially dangerous one because it was neither left wing or right wing, but privatised and apolitical. According to Mills, the problem with this situation is that these workers have no sense of their own interests as a class and will therefore simply follow the 'bloc or movement that most obviously seems to be winning.'[34]

This class is not only despised for its supposed lack of 'imagination' but is presented as the perfect raw material for a totalitarian society, a class incapable of independent action, which is simply waiting for a strong leadership to tell it how to behave. As Mills puts it:

> Since they have no public position, their private positions as individuals determine in what direction each of them goes; but as individuals, they do not know where to go. So now they waver. They hesitate, confused and vacillating in their opinions, unfocused and discontinuous in their actions... They are the rear-guarders. In the shorter run, they will follow the panicky ways of prestige; in the longer run, they will follow the ways of power, for, in the end, prestige is determined by power. In the meantime, on the political market place of American society, the new middle class are up for sale; whoever seems respectable enough, strong enough, can probably have them. So far nobody has made a serious bid.[35]

Mills does stress that this situation is the product of a mass society in which this class is denied power and simply consigned to the position of 'spectators' before the political stage. However, like so many other commentators of the period, Mills' discussion seems to slip frequently between presenting the situation of the class as the *effect* of the existing relations of power on the one hand, and as the *cause* of them on the other. The plight of the class, therefore, becomes merely 'pitiful rather than tragic',[36] and its members are presented as passive, masochistic victims rather than as heroic underdogs.

For example, he presents the media as one of the institutions through which such inequalities are generated, and claims that it produces 'a sort of psychological illiteracy'.[37] However, despite these criticisms, Mills suggests that the cultural condition of the new middle classes is not an *effect* of these media, but rather their *raison d'être*. He says:

> Popular culture pervades all classes of the American population, but perhaps, if only because of the age and sex differences, it grips the white-collar girl and the black-coated man most firmly. They are at the center of the high-school culture at which the mass media are targeted, and as a new lower middle class, they form an eager market for the gross output.[38]

Implicit within this statement is the suggestion that the mass culture of the period was not directed, as was often claimed, at the *lowest* common denominator, but rather at the middle or average, i.e. at the white-collar workers.

INTELLECTUALS AND THE FEAR OF THE MIDDLEBROW

The debates about mass culture that were so prevalent in the post-war period were frequently motivated by a fear not of mass taste but of the middlebrow. As we have seen, Boorstin criticised the *Reader's Digest* for its attempt to popularise more legitimate culture and, in a similar way, Macdonald's formidable critique of mass culture made it quite clear that he believed the real danger came from midcult or the middlebrow. As Macdonald argues:

> In these advanced times, the danger to High Culture is not so much from Masscult as from a peculiar hybrid bred from the latter's unnatural intercourse with the former. A whole middle culture has come into existence and it threatens to absorb both its parents. This intermediate form – let us call it Midcult – has the essential qualities of Masscult – the formula, the built-in reaction, the lack of any standard except popularity – but it decently covers them in a cultural figleaf. In Masscult the trick is plain – to please the crowd by any means. But Midcult has it both ways: it pretends to respect the standards of High Culture while in fact it waters them down and vulgarizes them.[39]

Midcult is dangerous precisely because it threatens the identity of art and its Other, mass culture, both of which loose their sense of integrity, outline and clear distinction from one another. Midcult not only creates a 'blurring of this line' between the two, but it threatens to engulf and 'absorb' them into itself.[40] It is a an 'ooze [that] is spreading everywhere.'[41] While the popular forms of the past were simply 'a parallel formation to High culture' that 'knew their place', the problem with midcult is that it is becoming 'the norm of our culture'.[42] In blurring the line between high and low culture, it threatens to obliterate them both and to replace them as the one and only form of culture in America.

If ever there were a force for conformity and homogenisation, it would seem, from Macdonald's description, that this was it. It is a force that respects no identities, no distinctions and no hierarchies. But it is not a foreign contagion that threatens an otherwise healthy American body. On the contrary: for Macdonald, 'there is something damnably American about Midcult.'[43]

Like others, then, Macdonald sees the real threat as lying in American capitalism, or rather in its application to the realm of culture. This mode of economic organisation, he claims, produces a situation in which the main criteria for the production of culture becomes the pursuit of profit, a situation in which the production of culture is rationalised like any other mode of industrial production and so churns out standardised works whose difference from one another is merely illusory. Produced by an industrial system, these works lack an 'author' whose vision is expressed through their art, and instead the works are 'fabricated by technicians hired by business men'.[44] They are 'manufactured rather than composed'[45] and hence lack all style and personality.

However, it is not just in the realms of production that rationalisation takes place. In order to secure a regular market for their goods, these cultural industries must also, it is claimed, rationalise and organise the audience. They not only standardise their own industrial output, but in the process, they seek to standardise the responses of the audience. Indeed, response becomes too strong a word, and Macdonald therefore favours the term 'reaction', which suggests that it is closer to a physical reflex than to intellectual contemplation. For Macdonald, the products of the cultural industries involve the 'total subjection of the spectator'[46] in which nothing is required of the audience, and all the work of interpreting and assimilating the material has already been done for them. The point is not simply that, as standardised products, these forms 'are easier to consume since one knows what's coming next,'[47] but rather that 'the spectator's reactions [are included] in the work itself instead of forcing him to make his own responses.'[48] The work 'predigests' everything so that not only is there no effort required on the part of the audience, but the reactions that they experience are not even their own and have been made for them by the work itself. The spectator has become a mere effect of the cultural industries and their products, and is subjected to both their demands and their conditioning.

The danger of this situation, according to Macdonald, is that it trains the population not to think of themselves as individuals, but to conform both to the image of the 'mass', in which everyone is the same, and to the systems of authority and power. The cultural industries (although this is in no way claimed to be a conscious intention on their part) train people to believe that by surrendering their own individuality and judgement, and by letting others think for them, the system will fulfil all their needs and satisfy all their desires. It trains them to repress their individuality and to defer to authorities.

Ironically, it is here that some of the contradictions of Macdonald's position become most apparent. Macdonald may present his complaint as one directed against a totalitarian system of authority and conformity but, like many other critics of the new petite bourgeoisie, it is instead a reaction against the threat that the middlebrow poses to the authority of intellectuals like himself. As a result, while Ross claims that the 'neo-aristocratic critique of mass culture ... as an extension of hyperdemocracy – the "political domination of the masses" (from below) – had, by this time, lost most of its political validity,'[49] this critique remained far more endemic than he acknowledges. However, it was no longer limited to the neo-aristocratic conservatives, and was therefore frequently disavowed even at the very moment that it was being employed.

For example, Macdonald stresses that it is capitalism and *not* the bad taste of the 'masses' that is responsible for mass and middlebrow culture. He claims that the cultural industries do not simply pander to the tastes of the audience, but that the taste for mass and middlebrow culture is a result of the fact that people have learned to like what they get given. As a result, Macdonald states that while 'objections to the giving-to-the-public-what-it-wants line are often attacked as undemocratic and snobbish … it is precisely because I do believe in the potentialities of ordinary people that I criticize Masscult.'[50] However, this statement rarely seems to coincide with Macdonald's other claims.

Macdonald rejects the possibility of trying 'to integrate the masses with high culture',[51] and claims that while 'there never has been a broadly democratic culture on a high level', this is 'not because the ruling class forcibly excluded the masses'. On the contrary, it is 'quite simply because the great majority of people at any given time … have never cared enough about such things to make them an important part of their lives.'[52] Of course, Macdonald never broaches the question of *why* it is that the majority of those people who *have* 'cared enough' should be from a specific class. Furthermore, he claims that 'the post-1750 public, lacking the taste and knowledge of the old patron class, is not only satisfied with shoddy mass-produced goods but in general feels more at home with them … because such goods are standardized and so are easier to consume'.[53] Here, a taste for mass-produced goods seems to come before the goods and not vice versa. Indeed, it is frequently the 'democratization of values' that is attacked by Macdonald or, in other words, the claim that everyone has a right to their own opinion. As Macdonald puts it, this 'process destroys all values, since value judgements require discrimination, an ugly word in liberal-democratic America. Masscult is very, very democratic; it refuses to discriminate against anything or between anything or anybody.'[54] Thus, according to Macdonald, while democracy may be may be 'desirable politically',[55] it is seen as a disaster for culture.

CONCLUSION

This intellectual critique of conformity is, however, only one deployment of the discourse in the period. The new middle classes themselves were engaged in struggles for distinction in which different sections opposed themselves to other sections through the discourse of conformity. What is more, this discourse of conformity was also deployed in a series of struggles over gender, race, region and other constructions of cultural identity. For example, not only did Philip Wylie attack gender relations in America by associating conformity with a 'feminization of America',[56] Betty Friedan also used the discourse of conformity to criticise 'the feminine mystique',[57] a critique that has been seen as the origin of second wave feminism. However, both Wylie and Friedan rely on an association between conformity and femininity,[58] even if they do so for wildly different reasons.

In studying the post-war period, then, we need to move away from the practice of recycling uncritically the assertions of individuals and groups that have claimed to present a unique challenge to a pervasive post-war conformity. Instead, we need to re-examine the cultural politics within which such claims were made and operated. Such a practice will not only provide a sense of the period that is far more complex than many existing accounts, but will also require us to be far more critical of those features that have often been championed by previous scholars. It requires us to question who is being Othered in these debates and who is attempting to establish their superiority and authority.

Notes

1. Barbara Klinger, *Melodrama and Meaning: History, Culture and the Films of Douglas Sirk* (Bloomington, Indiana University Press, 1994), p. 104.
2. Daniel Bell, *The End of Ideology: On the Exhaustion of Political Ideas in the* (Cambridge, USA, Harvard University Press, 1988), p. 35.
3. Andrew Ross, *No Respect: Intellectuals and Popular Culture* (New York, Routledge, 1989), p. 50.
4. Arthur M. Schlesinger Jr., *The Vital Center: The Politics of Freedom* (Cambridge, Riverside Press, 1949), p. 27.

5. See the discussion in Mark Jancovich, *Rational Fears: American Horror in the 1950s* (Manchester, Manchester University Press, 1996).
6. See, for example, Daniel Bell, *The Cultural Contradictions of Capitalism* (London, Heinemann, 1976), and Christopher Lasch, *The Culture of Narcissism* (New York, Norton, 1979).
7. See, for example, Alvin Gouldner, *The Future of Intellectuals and the Rise of the New Class* (New York, Seabury Press, 1979).
8. See, for example, Barbara and John Ehrenreich, 'The Professional-Managerial Class' in Pat Walker (ed.), *Between Labor and Capital* (Boston, Sound End Press, 1979), and Barbara Ehrenreich, *Fear of Falling: the inner life of the middle class* (New York, Pantheon, 1989).
9. See, for example, Pierre Bourdieu, *Distinction: A Social Critique of the Judgment of Taste* (London, Routledge, 1984), and R.W. Connell, *Masculinities* (Oxford, Polity, 1996).
10. For Schlesinger, 'freedom has brought with it frustration rather than fulfillment, isolation rather than integration' (p. 52) and, as a result, it requires a sense of responsibility on the part of the individual, a responsibility that entails the agony of moral decision-making. In contrast, totalitarianism is presented as a response to these 'freedoms' of modernity, and one whose seductive attractions are based on its promise of security and comradeship, in which the individual is 'freed' from responsibility by the discipline of the organisation. The totalitarian organisation, it is argued, spares its members from the agony of decision-making by telling them what to do and what to think.
11. William Whyte, *The Organization Man* (Harmondsworth, UK, Penguin, 1956), p. 48.
12. Whyte, *The Organization Man*, p. 8.
13. Whyte, *The Organization Man*, p. 365.
14. Whyte, *The Organization Man*, p. 9.
15. Whyte, *The Organization Man*, p. 48.
16. Whyte, *The Organization Man*, p. 53.
17. C. Wright Mills, *White Collar: The American Middle Class* (New York, Oxford University Press, 1951), p. xvii.
18. Mills, *White Collar*, p. xvii.
19. Mills, *White Collar*, p. xvi.
20. Mills, *White Collar*, p. xvii.
21. Mills, *White Collar*, p. 257.
22. Vance Packard, *The Status Seekers: An Exploration of Class*

Behaviour in America (Harmondsworth, UK, Penguin, 1959), p. 12.
23. Packard, *The Status Seekers*, p. 40.
24. Packard, *The Status Seekers*, p. 14.
25. Packard, *The Status Seekers*, p. 14.
26. Packard, *The Status Seekers*, p. 14.
27. Vance Packard, *The Hidden Persuaders* (Harmondsworth, UK, Penguin, 1957), p. 47.
28. Packard, *The Hidden Persuaders*, p. 216.
29. Daniel Boorstin, *The Image: or What Happened to the American Dream* (Harmondsworth, UK, Penguin, 1962), p. 13.
30. Boorstin, *The Image*, p. 141.
31. Boorstin, *The Image*, p. 11.
32. Boorstin, *The Image*, p. 11.
33. Elaine Tyler May, *Homeward Bound: American Families in the Cold War Era* (New York, Basic, 1988), p. 187.
34. Mills, *White Collar*, p. 353. Some critics of the period even accused this class and their 'status panic' of being responsible for the rise of the new right and of post-war anti-Communists such as Senator Joe McCarthy. See, for example, Daniel Bell, *The New American Right* (New York, Criterion), 1955.
35. Mills, *White Collar*, p. 353-4.
36. Mills, *White Collar*, p. xii.
37. C. Wright Mills, *The Power Elite* (New York, Oxford University Press, 1956), p. 311.
38. Mills, *White Collar*, p. 339.
39. Dwight Macdonald, 'Masscult and Midcult' in *Against the American Grain* (London, Victor Gollancz, 1963), p. 37.
40. Macdonald, 'Masscult and Midcult', p. 37.
41. Macdonald, 'Masscult and Midcult', p. 54.
42. Macdonald, 'Masscult and Midcult', p. 55.
43. Macdonald, 'Masscult and Midcult', p. 59.
44. Macdonald, 'Masscult and Midcult', p. 14.
45. Macdonald, 'Masscult and Midcult', p. 6.
46. Macdonald, 'Masscult and Midcult', p. 7.
47. Macdonald, 'Masscult and Midcult', p. 28.
48. Macdonald, 'Masscult and Midcult', p. 29.
49. Ross, *No Respect*, p. 52.
50. Macdonald, 'Masscult and Midcult', p. 11.
51. Macdonald, 'Masscult and Midcult', p. x.
52. Macdonald, 'Masscult and Midcult', pp. 72–3.
53. Macdonald, 'Masscult and Midcult', p. 28.
54. Macdonald, 'Masscult and Midcult', p. 12.

55. Macdonald, 'Masscult and Midcult', p. 34.
56. Philip Wylie, 'The Abdicating Male … and How the Gray Flannel Mind Exploits Him Through His Women', *Playboy* (November, 1956) and 'The Womanization of America: an embattled male takes a look at what was once a man's world', *Playboy* (September 1958).
57. Betty Friedan, *The Feminine Mystique* (New York, Dell, 1963).
58. See the critique of Friedan in Joanne Hollows, *Feminism, Femininity and Popular Culture* (Manchester University Press, 2000).

CHAPTER TWO

'Don't fight it. You can't whip Mickey Mouse.'[1] Disneyland's America 1955–59[2]

Emma Lambert

To all who come to this happy place,
Welcome.
Disneyland is your land.
Here age relives fond memories of the past
and youth may savour the challenge and promise of the future.
Disneyland is dedicated to the ideals,
the dreams and the hard facts
that have created America,
with the hope that it will be a source of
joy and inspiration to all the world.[3]
(© Disney Enterprises, Inc.)

On 17 July 1955 in Anaheim, south of Los Angeles, a new concept in leisure came into being with the opening of Walt Disney's Disneyland theme park.[4] Symbolic centre of attention was the dedication plaque at the park (text above), unveiled by Walt Disney. It was then, and is to this day, the first principal element that guests encountered upon visiting the park,[5] and the ideas contained within it illuminate the role played by the park within the politics and the culture of the Cold War. The plaque proposes a coherent relationship between the park and the nation, for Disneyland is dedicated to 'the dreams and the hard facts that have created America'. Yet, since Disneyland is to act as an ambassador of America to 'all the world', it also suggests a relationship between the park and the state.

Despite a plethora of Disney scholarship, little work focuses primarily upon Disneyland.[6] More surprising, despite the fact that the park was planned and constructed at the height of the early Cold War in the USA, no academic account exists that attempts to place Disneyland within this highly relevant and productive political and cultural context. In this chapter, through a reading of the narratives of Disneyland,[7] I will attempt to locate the park within the discourses of the Cold War and within the matrix of American nationhood and statehood during this time.[8]

DISNEYLAND'S AMERICA

Launched by the Truman Doctrine (1947) into an ideological conflict with the Soviet Union, the American nation was forced not only to discredit their enemy, the 'other', but also to seek to define a nationhood, a 'self'. The cultural atmosphere of the 1950s, charged by the politics of the Cold War, thus necessitated the phenomena of self-definition at all levels and in all areas of life.[9] These attempts to define and negotiate ideas of America and American-ness through all spheres of life became characteristic of this period.

In attempting to define the essence of nationhood in the present, recourse was made to the combination of the heritage of the past and the promise of the future. Literature on 'modernity' in the period stressed the importance of this interaction between past, present and future, and this was to achieve particular resonance within the newly charged cultural atmosphere. Michael Kammen, in particular, has noted these processes at work in post-war America.[10] Disneyland was no exception to either of these critical processes:

> [Disneyland's main theme] is a three-dimensional treasury of Americana of yesterday and tomorrow. There's the sentimental journey of the almost life-size stern-wheeler Mark Twain, the coon-skinned, stockaded actuality of frontier life; the serious, scientifically accurate foretaste of space travel and atomic progress – all adding up to what made us what we are today and pointing optimistically to the future.[11]

By presenting and interpreting the American past in Adventureland and Frontierland, and the American future in Tomorrowland, Disneyland entered into Cold War discourses of American identity and meaning of the nation in the present. It became, therefore, a definition in progress of the meaning of nationhood, produced at a time when it was of supreme political importance to attempt to define oneself (however (un)successful the end result) in contrast to a perceived enemy.

The discourses of the American past and future at Disneyland both worked within, and fused to form, discourses of contemporary Cold War America. Thus, at key points within the park, the concept of the American nation became displayed and consumed in a uniquely politicised Cold War manner. This may be characterised through several recurring modes of discourse, the most pervasive of which, 'freedom', will be examined here.[12] This cultural rhetoric, linked closely to the political rhetoric of the time, manifested itself in two slightly different, but related, ways: the notion of the freedom to consume and ideas of political freedom (from tyranny/to be democratic).

The importance of the idea of freedom within American political culture has been noted by many scholars.[13] In addition, with the advent of a major totalitarian power bloc after the war that was supposed to have rid the world of such phenomena, the discourses of freedom came to assume even greater poignancy. The importance of political freedoms was highlighted both in 'political' and 'cultural' texts throughout this period:

> I believe that it must be the policy of the United States to support free peoples who are resisting attempted subjugation by armed minorities or by outside pressures.[14]

> Liberty is not a means to a higher political end. It is itself the highest political end... A generous spirit prefers that his country should be poor and weak and of no account, but free, rather than powerful, prosperous and enslaved.[15]

Even the motto of Captain Video, star of children's television during the 1950s, proclaimed him 'champion of justice, truth and *freedom*'.[16] This expressly political concept of freedom was extended and intertwined with the related concept of *freedom to consume,* as symbolised by a cover picture from the *Saturday Evening Post* of 1959, which Karal Ann Marling describes:

> The American Dream was the topic of the *Saturday Evening Post*'s smugly archetypal cover of the summer of 1959. As a young couple dreams of their future together, its operative symbols appear in the starry sky above them, like the signs of the Zodiac, re-tooled by Madison Avenue.[17]

The cover displayed a plethora of consumer goods, from cars to music systems, a television and all manner of electrical appliances, the items that came to symbolise the emergent consumerism of the 1950s. Yet these items stood for something more than their actual or practical use value. Gottdeiner comments, 'They stood for something fundamental to the post-war understanding of national identity: a sense of *freedom*, of effortless ease, of technological mastery, modernity and access to conveniences formerly reserved for the very rich.'[18] Historian David Potter also traces the relationship between consumerism and democracy, illustrating the manner in which the public virtues of democracy were woven into the fabric of private life, into every sphere, even the choice of a brand new suburban kitchen.[19] The pinnacle of meaning for such notions came with the direct confrontation of Nixon and Khrushchev in 1959, at which the virtues of American freedoms triumphed over Communist tyranny through the medium of consumer choice: 'We hope to show our diversity and our right to choose. We do not want our decisions to be made at the top by one government official that all houses should be the same ... *let the people choose the kind of house, the kind of ideas they want* [my italics].'[20]

The political importance of capitalist culture and conspicuous consumption throughout the 1950s, symbolised by the 'Kitchen Debates', is nowhere more apparent than at Disneyland. Not only was Disneyland an economic godsend for Orange County and

Southern Californian tourism,[21] but it also treated its visitors to a 'shopping mall' and a leisure experience. The opening area of the park comprised a turn-of-the-century experience of consumption: Main Street USA contained such stores as an 'apothecary, ice cream parlor and bank, all open for business'.[22] Throughout the park, various corporate concessions and exhibitions not only kept the tills ringing but also advertised and contributed to an atmosphere of conspicuous consumption: 'A wonderland of brand names with a captive viewing audience of 5000000 people a year. That's the way ad-men look at Disneyland Park... More than thirty nationally advertised brand names are on display.'[23]

The freedom to consume was linked into the different areas of the park wherever possible. Over in Adventureland, those not braving the Jungle Cruise attraction could occupy themselves with some shopping: 'the Bazaar, or trading post, has shelves bulging with imports and curios from all the world's far places. The mood is one of unhurried browsing as visitors stroll from shop to shop in this unique indoor–outdoor market place.'[24] Even beyond the physical boundaries of the park, Disneyland was linked with a multitude of other products through advertising tie-ins: United Airlines highlighted their helicopter service to Disneyland, and the Insurance Company of North America claimed that dealing with them 'makes your everyday land as carefree as Disneyland.'[25] A wealth of other promotions, including token collecting, free gifts and so on, were run in conjunction with other businesses, particularly stores and supermarkets.[26] The park also produced large quantities of its own merchandise. An early issue of the *Disneyland News* afforded prime magazine space to a glossy two-page spread advertising Disneyland gifts (including a Davy Crockett outfit, a 'Junior Miss' beauty kit and a scenic Disneyland bracelet), available through mail order:

> Disneyland, California is more than an address, it's a dream come true ... a place of happiness. And a gift from Disneyland carries with it fun and fantasy that will never be forgotten. Each item described on these pages has been created by America's finest

> artists and craftsmen… Every gift from Disneyland is excitingly wrapped, bright with color, gay and festive as the Magic Kingdom itself.[27]
> (© Disney Enterprises, Inc.)

This text, which accompanied glossy colour photographs of the available gifts, not only described items, but also proposed a relationship between purchasing and dream, between the freedom to consume and true happiness. Thus, Disneyland provided, through cross-media interaction, advertising, marketing and promotion, a focal point for a whole network of conspicuous consumption and functioned ultimately as a paradigm of post-industrial capitalism. The close connections between capitalism and the political struggle against Communism meant that the park functioned, through its omnipresent consumerism, as a political statement, a symbol of the success of the American system.

Alongside these multiple discourses of consumption, a feature was planned for the park that would make the political implications of capitalism and its relationship to the concept of the American nation abundantly and starkly clear.[28] This feature, 'Liberty Street', made the links between Disneyland, consumerism, America and freedom particularly explicit, for it was intended to 'dramatise American heritage and the relationship of American business to the growth of the country'.[29] Early press information regarding the exhibit identifies clearly the importance of the notion of 'free enterprise' and links it consciously with greater discourses of freedom and the nation:

> A new addition to the Disneyland Park will dramatise the story of America's historical heritage and its relation to the concept of freedom of enterprise. Liberty Street, which will be a re-creation of a typical street in the Revolutionary War era, will depict the growth of American business and industry, relating the present scope of various businesses to their humble beginnings in the days of the founding of our nation. The principal theme of the new area will be the parallel development of America itself and the institution of free enterprise.[30]
> (© Disney Enterprises, Inc.)

Moments of narrative within the selective histories of Adventureland and Frontierland had privileged notions of freedom and exploration connected to the American frontier experience. The connections between consumerism and freedom had also been suggested throughout, but in the proposed exhibit of Liberty Street, these notions were to be made explicit, as areas of American political history and freedom were presented. The most important feature to consider in this respect is an element of Liberty Street known as 'The Hall of Presidents.'[31] This was announced to the public, in embryonic form, in the same press release that brought Liberty Street to the attention of the media:

> Dramatizing the most significant events in our American heritage, Walt Disney and his staff are also designing a number of tableau productions for Liberty Street which will give each spectator a living experience rather than just a show. Two large auditoriums are being planned. In the Hall of the Declaration of Independence, the framing, signing and proclaiming of this document, the most important state paper ever written, will be re-created. In the Hall of the Presidents of the United States, the history of our country will unfold through the eyes and deeds of all 34 presidents.[32]
> (© Disney Enterprises, Inc.)

The feature was also to include a carved stone model of the Capitol building in Washington and displays of its interior.[33] These plans to include a political exhibit at the park are important in several respects. Firstly, Liberty Street represents Disney's concern to educate as well as to entertain, and illustrates the politicisation of all manner of cultural experiences during these years. Secondly, by its very name and emphasis, Liberty Street singles out freedom as the most important defining characteristic of the American political psyche. In addition, the particular mode of representation selected – which asks visitors to share in the experience rather than simply observe it – invites visitors to share in a collective heritage, to affirm the narrative of their nationhood through the concept of freedom.

Finally, in the selection of 'key' historical events, the exhibit planned to highlight elements of American history that had particular resonance during the 1950s. Two years after the initial plans, the historical moments that deserved inclusion in the exhibit were outlined:

> Liberty Street will highlight the story of our American heritage and precious fought-for freedoms. Here will stand the Liberty Tree, about which the early patriots of Boston and other colonial towns rallied their courage and determination. Here will be created the Hall of Presidents, with the succession of our chief executives telling the progressive history of the United States, including Washington's Inaugural Address and Lincoln's Gettysberg Address. Shown in dimensional tableaux with life-size figures will be the signing of the Declaration of Independence and other momentous occasions. Heard will be the tolling of the Liberty Bell, sounding round the world as was the shot by Concord Bridge.[34]

Of the multiplicity of historical events and documents, the three that were singled out were of particular importance in creating and re-creating the political discourses of the Cold War. In the first instance, such documents and events had bequeathed to the nation a vocabulary and syntax of freedom with which the Cold War might be fought. Secondly, such terms and events were re-employed during the 1950s, as at Disneyland, to legitimate and reshape the terms of the conflict.

The Gettysberg Address deals almost exclusively with the notions of freedom and democracy. Given in the same year that Soviet tanks rolled into Hungary (1956), the invocation of government by the people, of the people and for the people, could hardly be more poignant. Likewise, Washington's inaugural speech highlights the centrality of the concept of free government to that of the successful form of the nation, and the Declaration of Independence takes a resolute stand against the tyranny that attempts to curtail such freedoms, for 'A Prince whose character is thus marked by every act which may define a tyrant, is unfit to be a ruler of a free people.'[35] Although there may be no direct relationship between the two, it is interesting and striking that such elements stressing 'freedom from tyranny' occurred in plans for a theme park exhibit simultaneously with the administration's development of 'Liberation' policy.[36]

Thus, Disneyland's collective narratives of past, future and present combined to create a particular conception of American nationhood that came, in turn, to direct both the park's commercial success and the role it might play in American public culture within the cultural apparatus of the American state.

DISNEYLAND: AMERICAN ICON

In his speech at the opening ceremonies, Governor Knight of California explained the importance of America to Disneyland (and, by implication, vice versa):

> Today is a wonderful day and all America is proud ... all this is built by American labour and American capital under the belief that this is a god-fearing and a god-loving country, and as we dedicate this flag now we do it with the knowledge that we are the fortunate ones to be Americans and that we extend to everyone everywhere the great ideals of Americanism.[37]

The interdependence of park and nation was illustrated further during the park's opening ceremonies, when the American flag was raised (as it still is to this day, every morning as the park opens) as the national anthem was played. Invited guests on the day included representatives not only from the world of entertainment, local community groups and major religions, but also from the state of California administration. Governor Knight's words expressed articulately the notion of the existence of a set of values, based around labour, capital, god and nation (the flag), which constituted the most desirable mode of existence, and as such, were worthy of export to other less fortunate peoples.[38]

Representatives of such 'less fortunate' peoples visited the USA as guests of the American government on a regular basis during the post-war period. As part of their itinerary, many visited California and Disneyland: 'Visitors to Disney's park have included eleven kings and queens, twenty-three presidents, prime ministers and other heads of state, and twenty-five princes and princesses... It is Disney policy that any guest of the United States is a guest of Disneyland.[39]

Such visits occasioned substantial media coverage both in the USA and abroad. In July 1957, the Prime Minister of Pakistan visited the park; his visit generated enormous worldwide press coverage and was also recorded by staff of the United States Information Service for inclusion in overseas newsreels and information films about the USA.[40] In December of the same year, the King of Morocco paid a visit to Disneyland. According to press reports, he 'arrived one morning in royal regalia, accompanied by a complete entourage. The king was given a brief formal tour, then departed shortly after noon for his Los Angeles hotel. Three hours later, he came back, wearing civilian clothes, and spent the rest of the day having fun with the other tourists.'[41] During 1957, a visit to Disneyland by several South American ambassadors made headline news, as newspapers reported the trip to the park by representatives of Bolivia, Ecuador, Columbia, Paraguay, Venezuela and Haiti.[42]

It is interesting to note the countries from which such visitors came, since they bear a coherent relation to the USA's security policy in the late 1950s. Following the Korean War, policy-making attention turned gradually away from Europe and towards other areas of the world that were considered vulnerable to the Soviet threat. The countries identified tended to be in the developing world and in South America.[43] It is, therefore, not surprising to find representatives from exactly those countries being treated to an American tour that included Disneyland. The administration was thus able to use the traditional diplomatic channels of overseas tours to promote relations not with all countries, but with the leaders of selected strategic areas. This manipulation of public relations is made even clearer in the case of Khrushchev's proposed visit to Disneyland in 1959.

Incomplete press release records at the Walt Disney Archives indicate that representatives of the State Department and the park's management were arranging a visit to Disneyland for the Soviet Premier. However, a press release in September announced, in response to press speculation, that no such visit had been confirmed, although Disneyland officials were prepared to handle a visit 'in the same manner that we have hosted other State Department tours of visiting Heads of State and top Foreign Government Officials who have toured the United States at the invitation of the President or the State Department.'[44] The proposed visit was, in fact, cancelled because the American government felt that Khrushchev's security within the park 'could not be guaranteed'.[45] That the Soviet premier's security could be assured in and about Los Angeles and yet not within Disneyland seems untenable, and one can only conclude that some other reason rendered Khrushchev an unsuitable visitor to the park at this time. Anecdotal insights into these events suggest that it was the Soviet premier himself who balked at the idea of visiting such a paradigm of capitalist dominance and American success:

> I asked Madame Khrushchev what they were planning to do after luncheon and she looked very crestfallen. 'We were so much looking forward to visiting Disneyland,' she said, 'but the police have told us that they cannot be responsible for our safety.' I passed this information on to Frank who reacted in typical fashion. 'Screw the cops,' he said, 'tell the old broad you and I'll take 'em down there this afternoon – we'll look after 'em.' I tactfully rephrased and then, via the interpreter, relayed this suggestion to Madame Khrushchev whose face lit up at the idea. She delved in her huge bag and scribbled a note to her husband which was despatched to the speakers' table. Khrushchev reacted angrily and signalled 'Nyet' to her with much wagging of a forefinger.[46]

Disneyland, therefore, could be included or excluded (by the USA or by their visitors) from high-profile itineraries in line with directions in foreign policy and international relations. A visit to, or exclusion from, Disneyland signalled far greater political meanings than simple (in)hospitality. Illustrating this further is the visit in 1956 of forty 'junior ambassadors to the United Nations', who visited the park as part of a visit to the USA:

> Nearly forty boys and girls from foreign nations scattered to the four corners of the globe will enjoy the highlight of their tour through the United States when they spend a whole day as guests of Disneyland on Thursday 25th November.
>
> Designated as Junior Ambassadors, one or two children from each of approximately twenty participating nations have been selected on the basis of intellectual achievement through a contest sponsored by Walt Disney Productions. The youngsters are from Argentina, Australia, Brazil, Chile, Denmark, Mexico, New Zealand, Peru, Portugal, Spain, Sweden, Venezuela, Norway, Switzerland and Austria.[47]
>
>

Once again, the choice of countries from which visitors were chosen is ideologically charged. By framing the visit within the guise of the United Nations, Communist and other undesirable nations could be excluded as 'common sense'. (This despite the fact that the political regime in Portugal at the time, although not Communist, could hardly qualify as a liberal democracy.[48]) In addition, a high-profile visit such as this affirmed the status of the United Nations (UN), and of the USA within the UN, and reaffirmed the importance of children and the family unit, linking with many other elements of contemporary ideology.[49]

The impetus for some of these official visits came from the Disneyland authorities themselves, always keen to create high-profile media coverage for the park. In 1956, a representative of the park, upon hearing of the forthcoming visit to the USA of Dr Sukarno, President of Indonesia, wrote to the Office of Protocol to 'extend an invitation to His Excellency and his entourage to visit Disneyland as out guest'.[50] For foreign dignitaries, the opportunity to visit Disneyland represented a chance to experience the world's leading leisure venue first-hand; for the park's administration, such visits offered valuable high-profile media coverage across the globe.

On other occasions, visitors themselves requested to see Disneyland. When the Soviet athletes who visited Los Angeles in 1956 were allowed to nominate a place of interest they wished to visit they chose Disneyland.[51] Although Khrushchev later refused to visit the park, the athletes were keen to see Disneyland perhaps because, as the premier global entertainment venue, it represented much of the world denied to them by the Soviet Union. The visit also caused an interesting political debacle, which offers further comment on the political importance and meanings of the park. *The Los Angeles Times* of 13 December 1956 covered the athletes' visit to Disneyland and photographed them riding inside the cages of the circus train, 'Casey Jr'. The photograph of the caged athletes was published in the *Times* that day. Unfortunately, the cage in which they were riding was labelled 'monkeys'. The incident provoked embarrassment and apologies from Disneyland, but also provoked a political cartoon that appeared in the *Los Angeles Times* the following day. The cartoon showed a scene in 'Satellite Dismaland', in which a giant gorilla clad in Soviet cap was shown inside a train cage entitled 'barbarism' and 'Hungarian Hatchet rule', as it trundled through a desolate, smoggy cityscape. Unintentionally, but not unimportantly, Disneyland had become entwined with direct cultural comment on the Cold War, the Soviet Union and the invasion of Hungary.[52]

The inclusion of Disneyland within the itineraries of many important foreign dignitaries accords it the importance of a national monument or museums akin to those along the Mall in Washington DC. It thus legitimised mass cultural forms within the elitist canon of 'suitable' public and state monuments. Such considerations link with broader debates throughout the 1950s regarding the meanings of culture generally and the value of new, popularised, mass cultural forms in particular, which sought the answers to the same questions of the legitimacy of certain cultural forms.[53]

Such visits also worked within discourses of the American nation and offered a particular expression and experience of the USA for consumption by VIPs and the world's media. Disneyland achieved the status of shorthand for the USA itself since it contained elements of, and reference to, multiple meaningful areas of American culture and politics. The visit of the junior ambassadors, after all, had been designed to show the youngsters 'the American way of life'. Positing a fluid notion of the state and of state apparatuses,[54] one is able to see how Disneyland (above all a successful commercial entertainment venture), through a working of ideas of American nationhood that made it accessible, acceptable and useful to a contemporary audience, was incorporated into narratives and expositions of statehood.

Thus, as has been demonstrated, Disneyland could be used as an American showplace – a kind of permanent 'world's fair' dedicated to the American nation and American values as defined during the early Cold War. Dramatising many essences of the American way of life in a uniquely entertaining way, Disneyland appealed not only to a domestic audience, but also transmitted notions of America to the far corners of the globe, acting as impromptu ambassador of America, and all it represented, to the rest of the world.

Notes

1. 'What you don't know about Disneyland', *San Francisco News* (Thursday, 4 July 1957), p. 1.
2. This chapter arises out of research completed for my unpublished M.Phil. thesis, '"Don't Fight It, You Can't Whip Mickey Mouse": Disneyland's Cold War 1955–1959' (University of Birmingham, 1998). Material from the Walt Disney Archives is reproduced by kind permission of Disney Enterprises, Inc. I would like to thank the committee of the Graduate Travel Fund at the University of Birmingham, whose generous award allowed me to complete the archival work for this chapter. I would also like to thank Dr Liam Kennedy and Dr Scott Lucas, whose comments and criticisms of this piece have been invaluable.
3. Disneyland dedication plaque, Disneyland theme park, Anaheim, California. © Disney Enterprises, Inc.
4. Similar ventures had existed prior to the Disneyland venture, some of which Walt Disney visited and consulted during the planning processes of his own park. However valuable and essential these precedents, Disneyland undoubtedly strove towards, and achieved, the scale and ambition of something that was entirely new. For further information on the precursors to the park, see any of the texts in the 'auteurist' section of note 6.
5. Disneyland in 1955 consisted of four 'lands' grouped around a central street, Main Street USA: Adventureland and

Frontierland sat to the left of Main Street, with Fantasyland straight ahead, and Tomorrowland to the right. Although some exhibits have been removed and newer ones added, many of the original features remain. A physical sense of the park can be obtained, without a trip to California, through a virtual tour of Disneyland. See 'Mark's Ultimate Disneyland Adventure', http://www.concentric.net/~Diznyguy/, which describes itself as 'a cyber stroll through the happiest place on earth', 'Quicktime Virtual Reality Tour', http://www.hojoanaheim.com/vrtour.htm, and 'Lairds' Virtual Disneyland Tour', http://www.donaldlaird.com/personal/disney/virtual/.

6. Existing studies of Disneyland fall into two distinct groups: 'auteurist' writing, which positions the park within a general chronology of Disney and his work and 'postmodern' writing, which considers the park in a more critical manner, usually through spatial theory. Auteurist studies include a large number of general surveys of Disney and his empire exist, some of which include Disneyland within the framework of other Disney enterprises. However, these texts do not present an in-depth analysis of the park, tending instead towards a narrative and contextualising approach. See, for example, Richard Schickel, *The Disney Version: The Life, Times, Art and Commerce of Walt Disney* (New York, Simon and Schuster, 1968), which is a good all-round introduction to the many facets of the Disney empire. Bob Thomas, *Walt Disney: An American Original* (New York, Simon and Schuster, 1976) is the standard biography of Walt Disney, sanctioned by the corporation. Marc Eliot, *Walt Disney – Hollywood's Dark Prince* (London, Andre Deutsch Ltd, 1994) is a recent and useful addition to Disney scholarship; Eliot's book examines the relationship between Walt Disney and the FBI, painting a less than flattering picture of 'Uncle Walt'. Christopher Finch, *The Art of Walt Disney* (New York, Abrams, 1973) is a folio book that includes many colour illustrations of artwork from the Disney films and some illustrations of the theme parks. Walt Disney Productions Ltd, *Disneyland – The First Quarter Century* (1979) is the corporation's own very flattering tribute to itself after twenty-five years. 'Postmodern' studies include less narrative and more critical readings of Disneyland, although these fall short of analysis of the park within a political context. Sharon Zukin, *Landscapes of Power: From Detroit to Disneyworld* (Berkeley, University of California Press, 1991) is an analysis of Walt

Disney World, with some mention of Disneyland, which looks at the parks within the contexts of urban studies. Eric Smoodin, *Disney Discourse: Producing the Magic Kingdom* (London, Routledge, 1994) is a useful text that deals with broader questions of networks of power and the production of meaning. Michael Sorkin, 'See you in Disneyland' in Michael Sorkin (ed.) *Variations on a Theme Park: The New American City and the end of Public Space* (New York, Noonday Press, 1992) pp. 205–232 provides an interesting look at the urban precedents for Disneyland, particularly the Garden City. Mark Gottdeiner, *Postmodern Semiotics: Material Culture and the Forms of Postmodern Life* (Oxford, Blackwell, 1995) is a concise and yet wide-ranging overview of much of the research on Disneyland, with an interesting semiotic analysis of the park. Finally, there are some works that attempt something slightly different. Karal Ann Marling, *As Seen on TV: The Visual Culture of Everyday Life in the 1950s* (London, Harvard University Press, 1994) attempts to contextualise the park within the culture of the 1950s, but largely ignores specific political context or discourse. Mark Langer, 'Why the Atom is our Friend: Disney, General Dynamics and the USS Nautilus', *Art History* 18:1 (1995), pp. 63–69 comes close to the kind of approach I wish to achieve in this chapter, although he is restricted in subject matter to a single exhibit at the park. Likewise, Maria Lydia Spinelli, 'Fun and Power: Experience and Ideology at the Magic Kingdom (Disneyland, California)' (unpublished Ph.D. thesis, University of Massachusetts, 1992) on experience and meaning at the park has been useful, although her methodology is that of a social scientist and her focus is chronologically later. Warren Susman, 'Did Success Spoil the United States? Dual Representations in Postwar America', in Lary May (ed.) *Recasting America: Culture and Politics in the Age of Cold War* (Chicago, University of Chicago Press, 1989), pp.19–37 attempts to consider some of the political implications of the park, but his analysis, although interesting, comprises generalised notions rather than in-depth analysis supported by specific evidence. Scott Schaffer, 'Disney and the Imagineering of Histories', http://garnet.berk.4050/ids-pomo.html utilises a more politicised reading, although concentrating specifically on themes of imperialist discourse within Disneyland, and avoiding the generalised narrative offered by Susman, somewhat over-restricts his analysis. Finally, Steven Watts, *The Magic Kingdom. Walt Disney and the American*

Way of Life (Boston, Houghton Mifflin, 1997) a recent study of the Disney empire, is compelling. This provides generally sound critical coverage of the entire Disney enterprise. Watts' chapter on Disneyland tells the story of the park and critiques elements of it as an 'evocation of national values', a 'distillation and reaffirmation of post-war American culture' and as 'steeped in the patriotic sensibility of the Cold War'. Yet no further or closer analysis is forthcoming. For example, although the point is well made that the Tomorrowland section of the park illustrates continued technological progress, no link is made between this and the important atomic aspects of the Cold War. Similarly, the importance of 'the family' is seen simply as a post-war social 'trend' rather than as an integral part of the political rhetoric of the Cold War. These points aside, Watts produces a study more critical than many, and provides a welcome addition to Disney scholarship.

7. It is my intention in this analysis to illustrate areas of Cold War discourse and to analyse them as they appear at Disneyland, i.e. to 'read' the park. Therefore, it is not the primary focus here to discuss the intentionality of the producers, although this is suggested indirectly throughout (it is examined at greater length in the thesis that this chapter is derived from). Neither do I intend to consider contemporary reception of these narratives – a lack of visitor response materials renders this an almost impossible task, and the focus here is that these elements are readings that exist within the structure of the park, regardless of direct producer intention or direct consumer reception.
8. The terms 'discourse' and 'narrative' are used in line with many recent studies of the culture of the 1950s, as they allow a fluid approach to the study of culture and politics through linguistic and communicative notions.
9. Scholars have increasingly examined the ideological elements of the conflict. See, for example, W. Scott Lucas, 'Campaigns of Truth: The Psychological Strategy Board and American Ideology', *International History Review*, 18:2 (May 1996); Alan Needell, 'Truth is our Weapon: Project Troy, Political Warfare and Government–Academic Relations in the National Security State', *Diplomatic History*, 17 (Summer 1993), pp. 399–420. The ideological nature of the Cold War combined with the fact that, for the most part, it avoided actual conflict, meant that the cultural became the front line for the creation and

maintenance of a vision of self and enemy within the USA With the 'war' as a hyper-real rather than an actual event, the signs and symbols of the conflict, manifested through cultural discourses, came to represent the reality of the conflict.

10. Michael Kammen, *Mystic Chords of Memory* (New York, Knopf, 1991), pp. 537–70 and 571–617.
11. James Liston, 'The Land that does away with Time', *Better Homes and Gardens*, XXXIV (February 1956), pp. 62–3.
12. Several other discourses of the Cold War, such as containment, family and religion, might also be examined fruitfully in relation to Disneyland, but for reasons of brevity, such terms are not included here. A more detailed exposition can be found in the thesis that this chapter is derived from.
13. Robert E. Lane, *Political Ideology* (New York, Free Press of Glencoe, 1962). Max Lerner, *America as a Civilisation: Life and Thought in the United States Today* (London, Cape, 1958). Sam Girgus, *The American Self: Myth, Ideology and Political Culture* (Albuquerque, University of New Mexico Press, 1981). All of these provide analyses of American political culture in general, with some reference to the Cold War.
14. George Kennan, 'Long Telegram', in David Rees, *The Age of Containment: The Cold War 1945–1965* (London, Macmillan, 1967), p.21.
15. Advertisement for Welch Grape Juice Company Inc., *Commentary*, 14:6 (December 1952), p.629.
16. J. Fried MacDonald, *Television and the Red Menace: The Video Road to Vietnam* (New York, Praeger, 1985), p.125.
17. Marling, *As Seen on TV*, p. 255.
18. Gottdeiner, *Postmodern Semiotics*, p. 140.
19. David Potter, *People of Plenty: Economic Abundance and the American Character* (Chicago, University of Chicago Press, 1954), p.135.
20. 'The Two Worlds: A Day-Long Debate', *New York Times* (25 July 1959). 'Encounter', *Newsweek* (3 August 1959) pp.15–17. A single transcript of the events of this day does not exist. Various newspaper accounts of events are available and, between them, provide most of the necessary information.
21. 'All this is bringing wide, cash-register-full smiles to the faces of businessmen. Lunchrooms and service industries are bursting gussets. Realty values, already high in tract-booming Orange County, have skyrocketed in the vicinity of Disneyland. Realtors estimate that values have at least doubled within a two-mile

radius of the super-amusement park.' John Grover, 'Oh what Disneyland is doing to Orange County', *The Mirror and Daily News* (Friday 10 June 1955), p.12. 'In the two-and-a-half years since the Disneyland opening, these ten million visitors have spent upwards of thirty-five million dollars in Orange County.' 'Orange County's Biggest Industry', *Orange County Industrial News* (January 1958), pp. 14–15.

22. Martin Deutsch, 'Argosy Travel Trails – Disneyland and Surroundings', *Argosy*, CCCLXII (April 1996), pp. 90–92.
23. Louis V. Thormann, 'For big Advertisers: New Wonderland', *Printers Ink*, CCLII (15 July 1955) pp. 24–7.
24. Disneyland First Anniversary Souvenir Pictorial (1956), Walt Disney Archives, 500 S. Buena Vista St Burbank, Los Angeles, California. © Disney Enterprises, Inc.
25. *National Geographic Magazine*, CXXIV (August 1963), pp.150–152 (advertisements).
26. Disneyland Scrapbook D1, Walt Disney Archives. Although the material is uncatalogued and unreferenced, this file contains numerous examples of Disneyland marketing policies.
27. *Disneyland News* 1:4 (October 1955), pp. 15–18. Walt Disney Archives. © Disney Enterprises, Inc.
28. Although this feature never appeared at the California park (it opened at Walt Disney World in Florida, renamed 'Liberty Square'), it appears prominently in the planning of Disneyland during the years 1955–59, and retains its essential features at the Florida site.
29. Press Release, Monday 12 November 1956, Disneyland Press Releases, Walt Disney Archives. © Disney Enterprises, Inc.
30. Ibid. © Disney Enterprises, Inc.
31. The Hall of Presidents did not actually appear at Disneyland until 1965, due to the technical problems involved in creating suitably lifelike audio animatronics figures. However, as with 'Liberty Street', since the planning took place during the era being examined, the final product retains many of the original features.
32. Press release, Monday 12 November 1956, Disneyland Press Releases, Walt Disney Archives. © Disney Enterprises, Inc.
33. Ibid. © Disney Enterprises, Inc.
34. Walt Disney, 'My Newest Dream', *American Weekly (Los Angeles Examiner)* (9 March 1958), pp. 6–8.
35. Henry Steele Commanger (ed.), *Documents of American History* 2nd edn (New York, F.S. Crofts and Co., 1941), p. 102.

36. Charles E. Bohlen, *Witness to History 1929–1969* (New York, W.W. Norton and Co. Inc., 1973), pp. 268, 310 and 319. Here, the author discusses his own role in the formation and execution of the policy.
37. Dateline Disneyland, Walt Disney Archives. © Disney Enterprises, Inc.
38. The literature on American exceptionalism is extensive. See, for example, Jack P. Greene, *The Intellectual construction of America: Exceptionalism and Identity* (Chapel Hill and London, University of North Carolina Press, 1993) and Frederick Merk, *Manifest Destiny and Mission in American History* (New York, Knopf, 1970).
39. Leo Litwak, 'A Fantasy that paid off', *New York Times Magazine* (27 June 1965), pp. 22–3.
40. Walt Disney Archives, Press Releases 1955–59. © Disney Enterprises, Inc. The press releases concerned with such visits carefully document those involved. In all cases, those involved included United States Information Agency staff. I have tried to obtain information regarding these visits from the State Department Archives, but my efforts to date have been unsuccessful.
41. Robert Cahn, 'The Intrepid Kids of Disneyland', *Saturday Evening Post*, CCXXX (28 June 1958), p. 119.
42. 'Foreign Envoys visit Disneyland', *Los Angeles Express* (Monday 15 April 1957), Walt Disney Archives, Disneyland clippings file No.14.
43. See Youosuke Nagai (ed.), *The Origins of the Cold War in Asia* (New York, Columbia University Press, 1975) and Mark S. Gallacchio, *The Cold War begins in Asia* (New York, Columbia University Press, 1988). Most of the standard reference works on this period note a change in policy direction following the Soviet explosion of the atomic bomb and events in China in 1950.
44. Walt Disney Archives, Press Releases 1959. © Disney Enterprises, Inc.
45. Ibid. © Disney Enterprises, Inc.
46. David Niven, *Bring on the Empty Horses* (London, Hodder and Stoughton, 1975), p. 244.
47. *Disneyland News*, 2:5 (November 1956), Walt Disney Archives. © Disney Enterprises, Inc.
48. Standard histories of Portugal cover the post-war period adequately. For example, see David Lander Raby, *Fascism and*

Resistance in Portugal (Manchester, Manchester University Press, 1988).

49. Several writers have identified other key areas of contemporary ideology, such as a commitment to the family unit, a resurgence in religious belief, and ideological containment, particularly of women. See, for example, Marling, *As Seen on TV*, which deals with the appearance of many of these ideas in areas of popular culture. Similar ideas and concerns also abound at Disneyland and are covered in the thesis that this chapter is derived from.
50. Copy of letter to Office of Protocol (4 May 1956), Walt Disney Archives. © Disney Enterprises, Inc.
51. Cahn, 'The Intrepid Kids of Disneyland', pp. 22–3.
52. *Los Angeles Times* clippings (13 and 14 December 1956), *Disneyland Scrapbook D4*, Walt Disney Archives. © Disney Enterprises, Inc.
53. The best collection of contemporary debates on the topic is Bernard Rosenberg and David Manning White (eds.) *Mass Culture: The Popular Arts in America* (Glencoe, Free Press, 1957).
54. For example, Louis Althusser's notions of Ideological State Apparatuses in addition to Repressive State Apparatuses. See *Lenin and Philosophy and Other Essays* (New York and London, Monthly Review Press, 1971).

CHAPTER THREE

Beauty shops and bouffants: the political uses of beauty, style and domestic space

Julie A. Willett

During the 1950s, a woman's beauty and style played an important role in the cultural politics of containment. Like suburban track housing and manicured lawns, trips to the neighbourhood beauty shop and a weekly wash-and-set helped reinforce a Cold War ideology that stressed consumption, complacency and women's domestic role. Yet while beauty shops and bouffants helped to define American womanhood and an ideology of containment, the beauty shop was also a site where competing discourses were produced and consumed. In particular, the beauty shop supported women entrepreneurs at a time when women were expected to be domestic-bound and provided operators and customers alike with the space they needed to challenge the gender and racial inequalities they faced in both their personal and political lives.[1]

This chapter will explore beauty shop culture – from the conversations to the coiffures – in both Euro-American and African-American communities. More specifically, I will examine how beauty shop culture simultaneously reinforced and undermined the dominant discourses that shaped Cold War politics. Whether located in the suburbs or cities, bathrooms or basements, the neighbourhood beauty shop not only flourished in the post-war era, but also offered women a unique opportunity to challenge the culturally prescribed roles that their beauty rituals and elaborate hair styles implied. In other words, while the chit-chat and gossip that characterised beauty shops defined them as female space, beauty shops also afforded women the chance to escape temporarily, or to collectively confront the problems of home, family and community.

According to historian Elaine Tyler May, post-war femininity created an 'aura of untouchable eroticism' that fit neatly into the informal policies of domestic containment. Because of its explosive nature, female sexuality was deemed a risk to national security. But, like atomic power, it too could be harnessed and controlled for peaceful domestic use. Even styles of dress seemed to complement domesticity's post-war demands. By the late 1940s, the carefree dress of the 1920s flapper was long gone, as were the shoulder-padded styles that evoked strength through the Depression and war years. Replacing such styles was a 'quasi-Victorian' look, complete with 'long wide skirts, crinolines and frills'. Styles that accentuated the female figure, argues May, were designed to lure men into the sanctity of marriage and the security of the nuclear family. Sex was reserved for the marital bed, and a 'fortress of undergarments', including stays, girdles and padded brassieres, pushed and pinched femininity into its respectful place.[2]

In a similar fashion, hairstyles were also undergoing significant change. In the 1920s, the bob offered a defiant and carefree look that challenged a number of boundaries. Not only were beauty shops scarce enough to compel women to frequent barber shops and hence intrude on one of the central locations of male culture, but the short boyish look of the bob also raised concerns about sexuality at a time when lesbian and gay subcultures were becoming more visible in American cities.[3] Similarly, the development of the African-American beauty industry, which thrived to a great degree from hair straightening techniques, engendered considerable controversy. While African-American women flocked to beauty shops and began purchasing a wide variety of beauty products, black leaders questioned any process that seemed to tamper too much with racial identity.[4]

By the 1950s, women's crowning glories were styled elaborately and held together tenuously with a stockpile of bobby pins and an impenetrable layer of hair spray that created not only a look that was decidedly feminine and ultimately untouchable, but also a style that contrasted with those from preceding decades. Unquestionably time-consuming, poodles, beehives and bouffants seemed to contain women's every move and suggested that even hair knew its proper place. Whether straightened or curled, elaborate hairdos often meant that beauty operators spent hours washing and untangling the previous week's do simply to prepare the hair for another round of styling. The popularity of such styles fitted well with a Cold War discourse that emphasised containment and a domestic-bound role for women. At the same time, these styles meant that the beauty shop became part of an unprecedented number of women's lives during the post-war period. Not only had the number of shops more than tripled since the mid-1930s but more working- and middle-class women were likely to frequent their favourite shops on a regular basis. Indeed, because such styles required frequent, if not weekly, visits to the beauty shop, women found themselves chained to what seemed like an endless beauty regime that absorbed what little time they had left over after caring for an increasing number of children and their other domestic chores.[5]

The neighbourhood beautician was also considered as frivolous as the styles she created. Since the development of the hairdressing industry in the early twentieth century, trade leaders have ignored the contributions of working-class women who opened shops in their bathrooms and kitchens. More specifically, the hairdresser was generally depicted as a white, middle-class male who catered not to chatty neighbours but to society's elite. The male hairdresser, with his white coat and pristine salon, was, in the eyes of industry leaders, the epitome of professionalism and stood in sharp contrast to the beauty operator who dyed hair green and singed scalps while trying to cook dinner and care for her unruly children. Even when women received formal training from a beauty school, they ultimately failed to meet definitions of professionalism. According to Barbara Melosh's study of nursing, professionalism implied whiteness and maleness. Hence, female-dominated occupations could not, by definition, be professional in stature.[6] For decades, hairdressing journals like *The American Hairdresser* even attempted to deny the pink-collar nature of the industry and ignored the contributions of women as well as the very existence of the black hair-care industry.[7]

Ironically, the conservative character of the Cold War, and its emphasis on domesticity, encouraged the hairdressing profession to accept the kitchen beautician on her own terms. Indeed, a booming economy and time-consuming hairstyles meant enough space for both the fashionable downtown salon as well as the kitchen beauty shop. Moreover, although the home beauty shop had long offered the kind of flexibility that women had insisted was necessary to meet all their household needs and chores, now it fitted into the profit equation of industry leaders who also envisioned a larger domestic ideology that embraced women's roles as wives, mothers and consumers.[8]

In the 1940s and 1950s, the National Hairdressing and Cosmetology Association (NHCA) for the first time embraced the domestic arrangement of the kitchen beauty shop as well as a larger Cold War ideology that equated women's proper roles with the home. The beauty shop, argued the NHCA in its publication *The American Hairdresser*, should create an atmosphere amenable to the needs of mothers and their children. The journal featured what the NHCA considered a 'new' kind of shop and a model for the industry: Maggie's Shop, located in Culver City, California. Maggie's Shop reflected everything that the NHCA had seemed bent on discouraging only decades earlier: a design arranged specifically to accommodate children and one in which the male expert was conspicuously absent. In particular, Maggie's Shop ignored boundaries that divided business from home. A play yard with a sand pile was constructed so 'tots may be left to play with complete safety while mother has her hair done'. Instead of chastising Maggie, the NHCA praised her and suggested other 'clever trick[s]', such as the one in which the customers' children were offered magnets to scavenge about the shop floor in search of stray hairpins. Most important of all, the neighbourhood shop was idealised because it 'created a friendly, informal relationship between salon and patron', a relationship the NHCA now understood as 'a potential business builder'.[9]

Yet while the beauty industry became intertwined with a larger domestic ideology, it also offered women more opportunities for entrepreneurship and thus the means to manipulate, if not challenge directly, a Cold War discourse that emphasised the home and motherhood. Four out of ten of all beauty operators were in business for themselves in the 1950s, and that number undoubtedly overlooked the thousands of beauticians who often advertised only by word of mouth. At the same time, most states did not prohibit home shops, which further encouraged women to supplement the family income with a clientele based primarily on their neighbours and other familiar faces. As a result, small owner–operator beauty shops flourished alongside the more cosmopolitan salons that were found in the most fashionable shopping areas.[10] Above all, female owners and operators were challenging the 1950s myth perpetuated by men like George Gallup and Evan Hill, who conducted a survey of 2300 women and insisted that the American woman was 'uninterested in either business or politics'.[11] Within the hairdressing industry, an unprecedented number of women were not only owning and operating their own shops instead of dedicating themselves full-time to their homes, husbands and families, but were also managing employees, negotiating business deals with other entrepreneurs, overseeing inventories, and cultivating and maintaining a clientele.

Whether or not a woman owned her own shop, the expansion of the industry after World War II produced a labour shortage, which meant better wages for beauty workers. In 1949, the average weekly earnings for a beautician was just over $27 a week. By the 1950s, most beauticians were experiencing an increase in their weekly earnings. According to the Women's Bureau in 1950, new beauty operators usually 'began at a relatively low salary, depending on locality and type of shop'. But in a year or two the operator could easily 'double her earnings by building up her clientele'. For example, one mid-western state reported that earnings for the 'average beautician were $35 to $50 weekly in 1950'. Four years later, beauticians with less than one year of experience earned $50 to $60 per week and experienced operators made from $75 to $100 per week, not including tips. In exclusive salons, hairdressers could earn more than a $150 a week. By comparison, the average wage for waitresses nationwide was $3 a day or $18 for a six-day week in 1953.[12]

The relatively high wages of some beauticians meant that some women were able to redefine their stereotypical roles within the context of the family economy. In the 1940s, a Polish-American woman, Virginia Martel, enrolled in a beauty school at a cost of $125. Martell attended beauty school classes each morning, while her husband watched their new-born baby. When she returned from school, he went to work, and she 'would do all the diapers which [she] had soaked the day before'. Martell recalled that 'between doing diapers and steaming bottles, and taking care of the baby, I would try to study very hard because I couldn't fail.' Martell's hard work paid off when she graduated with 'an 88 average' and 'set up a little shop for [her] neighbors'. For a 'dollar or two dollars' she would 'give a haircut, a permanent, or a shampoo and set' so she could 'make extra money'. No sooner had she opened her shop, than her husband was 'taken into the service'. While he was gone, Martell explained, 'the government allowed me $100 per month'. By the time her husband returned from the service, their son was two years old and, with the help of her beauty business, she had saved $1000. For the next few years, Martell continued to work as a beautician and to increase her savings. The family moved several times, and each time they had to settle for a basement apartment until the savings from her beauty shop amounted to the sizeable sum of $3500, enough for a down payment on their first home.[13]

The beauty shop was thus not simply about idle gossip or an endless beauty regime. Nor did the beauty shop simply promote a Cold War mentality that devalued women's contributions and defined them as domestic-bound. In their beauty shops, and through their everyday trials and tribulations, women used their businesses to strengthen their roles in the family economy and to become enterprising entrepreneurs. In the process, they not only helped reshape the image of the industry but also produced a competing dialogue that defied their narrowly prescribed roles as mothers and housewives.

Like their Euro-American counterparts, African-American women in the 1950s also favoured hairstyles that seemed to emphasise conformity and artificiality. Yet even while these styles seemed to downplay any political sentiments and contrasted sharply with the Afro and cornrows – styles that would soon become potent symbols of black pride – the ways in which black women used their shops suggested anything but complacency.[14] In particular, beauty shops provided a means to challenge a dominant racial status quo that insisted that African-American women occupy the lowest paid jobs, and receive the fewest educational opportunities and the least adequate health care. Thus, a black woman who owned her own business and became a successful entrepreneur was not simply calling into question a Cold War domestic ideology that embraced the image of the happy housewife, but was confronting directly a system of apartheid that challenged her daily existence.

With relatively few independently owned businesses, African-American beauty shops, no matter how meagre, often provided the basis for an entire black community's post-war expansion. Hazel Foster 'was the first person in Tippah County [Mississippi] to own a telephone in the early '40s', which meant she played a decisive role in her community's life. 'I used to run messages around for the neighborhood', she recalled. In the 1940s, Foster's Beauty Salon offered primarily 'pressing and curling'. The services combined brought in less than seventy cents per customer – 'A press was $0.25, and it cost $0.35 for a thermal curl,' – and the work was labour-intensive. 'We didn't even have hot water then. We would heat water on a hot plate, and recline the client in a big bowl of warm water to wash her hair.' Yet despite her humble beginnings, Foster's small shop eventually grew into an impressive enterprise that offered not only a variety of hairstyles, cuts, facials and even nail services, but also expanded to include 'a motel, day-care center, laundromat, funeral home, dormitory for the beauty college and a barber college'. Perhaps most significant of all, as of 1988, her salon was still 'the only black-owned business in Sherman, Mississippi'.[15]

Indeed, there were so few black-owned business in communities that African-American hairdressers not only fulfilled a variety of roles that went well beyond dressing hair, but offered a certain kind of trust that African-American women could rarely find in other institutions. In 1946, Alice M. Murray of Washington, DC was working as a domestic when she decided to attend beauty school at night, a decision that changed her life dramatically. Her training eventually led to her own business, Alice's Beauty Salon, a business that she described as being open virtually around the clock. 'We did not have closing hours then. We took as many as four customers as early as six o'clock a.m. before they went to work, and as many as ten in the evening after work.' The doors of her business never really closed because she cared for her customers and their various needs night and day. Her thirty-six years as a beauty operator taught her that 'beauticians have to be more than hairdressers'. While they may earn their money dressing hair, Murray insisted that they also had to be 'hair doctors, advisors, good listeners, relaxation therapists and more'. According to Murray, the little conversations so easily dismissed as mundane helped women who needed to escape or confront the pressures of home, family and work. 'Often, when women are upset,' she found, 'they will either go shopping or go to the hair parlor seeking relief.' But concern for a customer's welfare did not stop at the shop's front door, she insisted. Instead, for Murray, 'being there' for a customer involved 'a wide range of services', because she was always 'concerned about [the] customers' well-being', a concern that created intimate bonds between the beauty operator and her customers and defined the essence of hairdressing.[16]

Solving community problems and challenging the racial order has also meant looking out for future generations. While *The American Hairdresser* in the 1950s encouraged Euro-American hairdressers to build up their businesses by targeting teenage patrons, African-American beauticians recognised the teenager market as a political means to inspire a kind of inner strength that black youth needed to confront racism throughout their lives.[17] Lulline (Jackie) Long of Birmingham, Alabama, began her business, the Cannolene Cosmetic Company, by going 'door-to-door' until she had saved enough for a two-storey building, which housed the Cannolene store, her beauty school and salon. According to her husband Robert, 'she had the first beauty salon in our house' where she taught beauty culture and 'did hair – what you call the marcel [wave]'. Robert recalled that Parker High School girls from 'up the street … would stop by to get their hair done'. And Jackie would also 'bring boys in off the street and cut their hair for free – just so she could get a chance to talk to them … about staying out of trouble, about making something of themselves, and about God'. Jackie Long's success and generosity made her famous, and she was noted for the money she donated to the community. She founded the Youth Development of Birmingham, a place 'where arts, crafts and dance' are taught to African-American youth. Long also donated generously to summer recreation programs designed 'to help young people gain a direction in life'. Education was also one of her top priorities. Over the years, she gave emotional and financial help to 'countless thousands of children and young adults' in order that they 'receive education and achieve their life goals'. Her beauty shop even challenged Jim Crow education by including an unexpected library that housed an extensive collection of African-American history books and 'other treasures'.[18]

As both Lulline Long and Alice Murray's experiences suggest, the beauty shop not only provided a number of valuable services to their communities, but could also play an important role in raising consciousness. In particular, it provided the means and the opportunities to challenge an ideology of containment that meant not only limited access to good jobs and education but also opposition to any and all social reform efforts. As Manning Marble explains, 'The impact of the Cold War, the anti-Communist purges and near totalitarian social environment had a devastating effect on the cause of blacks' civil rights and civil liberties … [and] the paranoid mood of anti-Communist America made it difficult for any other reasonable reform movement to exist.'[19] Thus, it was no historical accident that beauty operators were found occupying key positions in grass roots struggles for civil rights. Ella Martin, who started the Poro Beauty College in Atlanta and the Georgia Beauty Culturalist League, was involved in volunteer work and voter registration drives. Beauty shops, Martin explained, were used 'to get them [her customers] interested in voting and to ... educate them to go to the polls to vote'.[20] Over the next two decades, the beauty shop's role in the civil rights movement would only gain strength. In the early 1950s, Bernice Robinson's political activism had already 'turned her Charleston beauty shop into a political outpost'. 'In 1951 or '52,' Robinson recalled, 'Joe Brown took over the NAACP [National Association for the Advancement of Colored People], and that's when we really started making something of the Charleston branch... In fact,' she boasted, 'we raised membership from three hundred to way over a thousand.' She admitted that sometimes she was 'working so hard getting people to register to vote that I would leave people under the dryer to take others down to the registration office to get them registered'.[21]

Indeed, beauticians' economic independence provided the wherewithal that community leaders needed to challenge directly the racial status quo. In the mid-1940s Myles Horton, who organised and directed the Highlander Folk School in Monteagle, Tennessee, which was designed to bring blacks and whites together to challenge segregation, explained the importance of beauty operators in the fight for civil rights. According to Horton, 'what you had to do in the pre-civil rights period was to find black people who for the most part were in situations where they weren't too dependent on white people. Otherwise, they would lose their jobs for coming.' And it was for this reason, Aldon Morris argues, that the civil rights movement attracted black ministers, funeral home directors, union members, independent small farmers and, of course, beauticians. According to Horton, beauticians were respected not only because they were entrepreneurs, 'small businesswomen, you know', but because 'they were usually better educated than other people, and most of all they were independent. They were independent of white control.' It was this connection between independence and beauty shops that inspired Horton to run workshops at Highlander 'just for beauticians'. Organising beauticians raised few suspicions, since most people assumed that Horton's interests were strictly vocational. 'They thought that I was bringing these beauticians together to talk about straightening hair or whatever the hell they do.' Instead, he insists, 'I was just using them because they were community leaders and they were independent.' And this is why, Horton explained, 'we used to use beautician's shops all over the South to distribute Highlander literature on integration'.[22]

Throughout the post-World War II era, beauty shops helped Euro-American and African-American women challenge the dominant politics of Cold War domestic containment. Despite the popularity of hairstyles that fitted well with a Cold War discourse that emphasised containment, the day-to-day problems and obstacles beauticians faced helped transform their beauty shops into important sites of resistance and opportunity. Indeed, the beauty shop provided women with the space to renegotiate their familial roles and their contributions to the family economy and their communities. At the same time, beauty shops played a profoundly influential role in the civil rights movement. The success of the beauty shop reflected its status as a kind of 'halfway house'.[23] Unlike the Church and other institutions, the beauty shop was less visible and thus provided the means to challenge more safely the racial status quo without the added pressure that more prominent institutions faced. In particular, the beauty shop's political use was less visible to whites. On the one hand, the predominance of the small neighbourhood shop, its one or two operators, and an informal atmosphere ensured that the hairdressing industry would remain associated with the home and domesticity, despite the number of different roles that beauticians and their shops played. On the other hand, the beauty shop was, for the most part, an exclusively female culture, which meant that most men would remain oblivious to what went on in beauty shops and continue to dismiss the relative importance of beauty shop culture. As such, the beauty shop helped nurture cultures of resistance that reshaped the politics of containment into a style that reflected rather than undermined the uses of domestic space.

Notes

1. On post-war images of womanhood and domesticity, see Elaine Tyler May, *Homeward Bound: American Families in the Cold War Era* (New York, Basic Books, 1988); Stephanie Coontz, *The Way We Never Were: American Families and the Nostalgia Trap* (New York, Basic Books, 1992); and Joanne Meyerowitz (ed.), *Not June Cleaver: Women and Gender in Postwar America, 1945-1960* (Philadelphia, Temple University Press, 1994).
2. May, *Homeward Bound*, pp. 110–13.
3. Christina Simmons, 'Companionate Marriage and the Lesbian Threat', *Frontiers*, IV:3 (1979), pp. 54–9.
4. Noliwe M. Rooks, *Hair Raising: Beauty, Culture, and African American Women* (New Brunswick, Rutgers University Press, 1996), pp. 80–81.
5. On the increasing number of beauty shops and the regularity of the standing appointment, see 'Vogue Survey Shows High Beauty-Shop Attendance', *The American Hairdresser* (January 1952), p. 54; 'The Shop With Once-A-Week Customers', *The American Hairdresser* (July 1951), pp. 62, 83 and 34; 'Memo From the Editorial Staff – The Breck Survey', *The American Hairdresser* (July 1953), p. 33; and 'Employment Opportunities for Women in Beauty Service', *Women's Bureau Bulletin* No. 260 (1956), pp. 2–3, US Department of Labor.
6. Barbara Melosh, *'The Physician's Hand': Work Culture and Conflict in American Nursing* (Philadelphia, Temple University Press, 1982), p. 20.
7. For examples of trade leaders emphasising the importance of men in the industry, see Nathan E. Jacobs, *NHCA's Golden Years* (Racine, USA, Western Publishing Company, 1970), pp. 5–6.
8. Robert R. Hoffman and Herbert S. Rosen, 'Two Views on the Shortage of Operators', *The American Hairdresser* (October 1952), pp. 48–9 and 73; and 'Memo from the Editor', *The American Hairdresser* (May 1952), p. 31.
9. 'For Profit – How She Does It!', *The American Hairdresser* (September 1951), p. 59; and Avis Splies, 'Babies Keep Customers Away ... Here's How Babies Can Bring Them In', *The American Hairdresser* (October 1951), p. 34.
10. *Employment Opportunities for Women in Beauty Service*, pp. 2–3 and 12–13.
11. For a discussion of this 1950s myth, see Alice Kessler-Harris, *Out to Work: A History of Wage-Earning Women in the United States* (New York and Oxford, Oxford University Press, 1982), pp. 301–2.

12. *Employment Opportunities for Women in Beauty Service*, p. 30; and Dorothy Sue Cobble, *Dishing It Out: Waitresses and their Unions in the Twentieth Century* (Urbana and Chicago, University of Illinois Press, 1991), p. 118.
13. Virginia Martel, Oral history Collection Chicago Polonia, Chicago Historical Society, MAR-106 (1–2), 24–7.
14. In her autobiography, Assata Shakur describes the meaning of the Afro: Assata Shakur, *Assata: An Autobiography* (Chicago, Lawrence Hill Books, 1987), pp. 31 and 174–5.
15. 'Hazel Foster Proves That "You Reap What You Sow"', *Shoptalk* (Fall 1988), p. 11.
16. Alice M. Murray, 'Reader Talk', *Shoptalk* (Spring 1985), p. 12. For a discussion of women's culture and the ways it can foster 'a sphere of freedom', see Patricia Hill Collins, 'Learning from the Outsider Within: The Sociological Significance of Black Feminist Thought', *Social Problem*, 33:6 (December 1986), pp. 15–32.
17. Lillian Blackstone, 'My Entire Business is Teens!', *The American Hairdresser* (September 1948), pp. 62, 64 and 92.
18. 'Legends of Cosmetology – Lulline Long: Selling Care and Concern', *Shoptalk* (Spring 1985), p. 111.
19. Manning Marable, *Race, Reform, and Rebellion: The Second Reconstruction in Black America, 1945–1990* (Jackson, University of Mississippi Press, 1991), p. 18.
20. Clifford M. Kuhn, Harlon E. Joy and E. Bernard West, *Living Atlanta: An Oral History of the City, 1914–1948* (Athens and London, The University of Georgia Press, 1990), p. 110.
21. Elliot Wiggintone (ed.), *Refuse to Stand Silently by: An Oral History of Grass Roots Social Activism in America, 1921–1964* (New York, Doubleday Dell Publishing Group, 1992), pp. 245–6.
22. Aldon D. Morris, *The Origins of The Civil Rights Movement: Black Communities Organizing for Change* (New York, The Free Press, 1984), pp. 139–40.
23. On the idea of a 'halfway house', see Morris, *The Origins of The Civil Rights Movement*, pp. 139–40.

CHAPTER FOUR

Zoot suit: breaking the Cold War's dress code

Candida Taylor

Containment culture's surveillance of citizen conduct for any signs of deviance made looking respectable a necessity. Clothes became external evidence of political intent. When *Life* magazine ran fashion spreads on the American look – Parisian styles adapted to suit the American woman's sensibilities – fashion had become aligned with national values.[1] Yet in the midst of this anxiety to be seen to conform, a new group was emerging, eager for ways to distance themselves from the mainstream. A nascent youth culture, in its desire to rebel against parents and the parent nation, seized upon clothes as the best means of proclaiming their rebellion. They adapted a style that had made its debut on the street nearly a decade earlier during World War II. This was a look rich in subversive meanings, which, owing to its specific history, announced loudly and proudly its disloyalty to the nation. The zoot suit with its legacy of un-Americanism and its connotations of racial and cultural otherness was the one style that could, even by its merest suggestion, profoundly shock the mainstream.

The zoot suit consisted of a drape jacket that reached down as far as the knees with wide lapels and broad shoulders 'padded like a lunatic's cell' as described in hip talk. The trousers were high-waisted with 'reat pleats', very baggy on the leg but tapered at the ankle.[2] The suit was worn with a very long key chain and often a crucifix or medallion necklace over the tie. To complete the look, the hair was the pompadour, a relatively long haircut for men, greased into a quiff at the front and combed into a duck's tail at the back. The flick-knife was kept in the hair, the thickness of the hairdo providing a secure hiding place for the weapon.

The zoot suit was a display of excess. It was fashion taken to its limits. This excess was where the style worked: excess is prized; it is vied for. The suit's exaggeration was based on a sense of outdoing anyone else's attempt. Its essence was of trumping other people's extravagance, of 'outcooling' others. Not only was the suit large in its cut, but it was worn with a large attitude, a quantity of bravado that presented the potential of violence. This violence was incorporated into the style of the hipster rendering it aesthetic. Flick knives, as potent symbols of masculinity, were worn in the hair like vicious bobby pins. The knives were used in a typically feminine manner to adorn the hair, keeping the greased locks in place. The wearing of the zoot suit was a rebellion, a transgression of gender boundaries. It hinged on tough, mean men adorning themselves.

According to George Lipsitz, the zoot suit became 'a symbol of rebellion' for middle- and working-class whites during the 1950s.[3] The style originated in 'black and Chicano working-class communities filtered up to set the pace for middle-class groups, especially youth'.[4] In the stifling atmosphere of Cold War containment, youths in the 1950s began to look outside their culture for alternative ways of expressing their individuality. Having grown up within the post-war climate of unparalleled consumer wealth, teenagers were endowed with a new measure of autonomy. They had their own money to spend without necessarily having to earn a living, and thus could choose to reject the values of their parents and community by looking elsewhere for cultural styles. 'By wearing the zoot suits,' suggests Lipsitz, 'young people identified with the dress of the poor rather than the rich, and flaunted their alienation from the surrounding culture.'[5]

In 1956, Elvis Presley appeared on the Milton Berle show wearing a zoot suit. With his infamous and unruly ducktail hairdo, Elvis sported the corresponding outfit: the oversized jacket and loose but pegged pants. As Karal Ann Marling explains, the voluminous cut of the zoot suit actually emphasised his provocative pelvic gyrations to the extent that it provoked a mob of screaming female fans with lustful motivations.[6] Elvis was an illustrious dresser with a particular penchant for assuming black and Hispanic dress styles, as much as those groups' musical styles. His adoption of the zoot suit, and the female reaction to it, probably popularised it among his white, teen audience. In a retrospective look at the fifties, the film *Grease* (1978) focuses upon the 'greaser' of the 1950s, the style that was based clearly on that of the zoot suit, notably the ducktail haircut. In *Grease*, this style is the mark of nonconformist youth. The zoot suit style here clearly signifies the subversiveness of a youthful rebellion against the conformist codes of containment culture.

As Dick Hebdige observed, style is a form 'of intentional communication', a non-verbal means of expression. Getting dressed each morning is a daily act of self-invention. The wearer positions themselves within various codes even if they are no more complex than 'the expression of normality as opposed to deviance'.[7] As such, no item of clothing is innocent; all garments bring with them associations upon which the individual will be judged. Violating the accepted style codes has the potential to shock and antagonise, as such behaviour threatens the cohesion upon which social order is based. In the case of the zoot suit, white youths positioned themselves within the garments' history. By adopting that form of dress, they (sub)consciously adopted a set of values that were not of their own making. The style may have been adapted and appropriated by whites during the Cold War as a form of resistance to the prevailing containment culture, but the zoot suit already held an undeniable political power. Its symbolic power was such that the style had hitherto incited servicemen to assault the wearers, culminating in the Zoot Suit Riots of June 1943. These riots iconised the suit as a marker of difference, probably bringing it to the attention of white youth and leading them to appropriate it in the first place.[8]

The style was revived in the 1950s by mainstream white youth in their desire to cast themselves as marginal to the Cold War culture. They probably chose the zoot suit because its innovators, the *pachucos*, were real outsiders. The pachucos' history is vital to understanding the significance of the zoot suit's style and the set of values that came to be attached to it during the 1950s. The *pachucos* were the male Hispanic dandies who emerged on the streets of East Los Angeles in the final years of World War II. The zoot suit was an articulation of the their defiance of mainstream North America and its war effort. It was labelled by the press and the authorities as the 'badge of delinquency'.[9] It was a confrontational style that asserted the pachucos' ethnic differences, whilst simultaneously distancing them from their Mexican backgrounds. During wartime, when difference was to be avoided and conformity to be cultivated at all costs, the zoot suit proclaimed its absolute otherness from all sides and revelled in it. The style drew its inspiration from various directions to form a web of interplaying ironies. It took the established style codes of respectability and masculinity and customised them, enhancing them to their logical limits in order to make a mockery of the values they communicated.

The zoot suit had been worn by a group of people who occupied a specific position within 1940s America. The *pachucos* were young, second-generation Mexican-Americans who were held responsible by the press for the wave of juvenile crime that swept the city of Los Angeles during the war years.[10] The Los Angeles Police Department (LAPD) made pronouncements about Mexican-American youths being biologically disposed towards violence since they were descended from the bloodthirsty Aztecs. Captain Ed Durán Ayres, spokesperson for the Foreign Relations Bureau of the LAPD stated that, whilst the Caucasian delinquent was inclined to fisticuffs, his Mexican counterpart was compelled to 'kill or at least to let blood'.[11] Such prejudices held by the authorities, along with factors such as poor education, segregation in public places and lack of employment opportunities, were more likely to have fostered *pachuquismo*.

Whilst it was poor schooling and holding criminal records that kept many *pachucos* out of the armed services, the majority were actually dodging the draft. Attitudes to war were primary factors in defining *pachuquismo*.[12] In their desire to style an identity that had nothing to do with nationality, they rejected the war effort wholeheartedly as of no concern to them. Such 'degenerate' behaviour of draft dodging, dope smoking and foppish attention to their clothes incurred the wrath of the broader Mexican-American community who saw the *pachucos* as giving Mexican-Americans 'a bad name'.[13] Some publicly active Mexican-American figures believed that serving in the armed forces was the saving grace for the Mexican-American and would bring about the integration of the Mexican-American into American society. The services' ability to iron out differences between individuals and turn them into standardised soldiers, 'dressed all alike', was believed to have 'given many of our shy, inferior feeling Americans of Mexican descent a chance to learn something, a chance to fit into the scheme of things, a chance to belong'.[14] For the *pachucos*, social redemption was worthless if it came at such a cost to individual freedom. They styled their differences using the zoot suit as 'the means through which that difference was announced'.[15]

Personal behaviour had national implications during the war. The *pachucos'* belligerent assertion of difference from the mainstream constituted un-American activity, but it was also their inactivity that was deemed unpatriotic. Whilst good American citizens rallied around putting their backs into the national war effort, the *pachucos* withdrew into their own insular culture, displaying total disregard for what was going on around them. They hung out in gangs, speaking their own language called *Caló*, a hybrid form of Spanish derived from the gypsy tongue.[16] They did not demonstrate a good work ethic;[17] in fact they exhibited a demeanour of languid detachment, enhanced by their use of marijuana. Work had no place in defining their identity. Their identity was based on display rather than their role within the machinery of national production, so crucial during a time of war. The only way the *pachucos* showed effort was in their dress. The distaste that servicemen and civilians had for the *pachucos'* suits and hairdos is evident from the violence that occurred during the Zoot Suit Riots.

In early June 1943, disturbances broke out in East Los Angeles, the Hispanic *barrios* of the city. Mobs of sailors and marines began scouring the streets in fleets of hired taxis, looking for zoot suiters to beat up, supposedly in retaliation for attacks upon their number by 'zooters'. If no candidates were found, they would storm into movie theatres and drag any young males they perceived as zoot suiters from the auditorium, taking them outside to strip them of their offending garments and cut their pompadour hairdos. Eyewitness accounts report that the attacks were unprovoked and actively encouraged by crowds of observing civilians.[18] Los Angeles police officers did not intervene in the assaults but looked on with approving eyes. After being brutally assaulted and publicly humiliated, the zoot suiters were then arrested for disturbing the peace.[19]

Public opinion was hyped up and orchestrated by the press who termed the riots the 'Zoot Suit War'.[20] In their reportage, the issue was clear cut. On one side were 'Uncle Sam's fighting men' and on the other was the enemy: the delinquent mob of zoot-suited gangsters responsible for terrorising innocent civilians.[21] The servicemen's actions were reported as a righteous 'clean-up' campaign to put a stop to the zooter crime wave that had been sweeping the East Side. Zoot suiters, the *Herald and Express* reported, had explicitly threatened to kill LA policemen, and the headlines blazed inflammatory slogans announcing 'Zooters Threaten LA Police' and relayed the message of an anonymous telephone call to police headquarters, which had stated: 'We're meeting 500-strong tonight and we're going to kill every cop we see.'[22] The servicemen were reported to have behaved with the utmost military decorum. Their attacks on *pachucos* were described as organised offensives with men moving in 'precise platoon drill' going in, not with the intention of being violent, but to deprive the zooters of their 'crude weapons'.[23] The *Examiner's* partisanship went as far to insist, in a burst of citizen outrage, that 'LA Police Must Clean Up LA Hoodlumism'.[24]

The events of the Zoot Suit Riots were remarkable for the fury and violence that clothing alone provoked. In the words of Stuart

Cosgrove, the Zoot Suit Riots were about 'style warfare'; uniformed US servicemen assaulting *barrio* dandies dressed to disrespect the American values of the moment. What is remarkable is that the lines of demarcation between people of the same nationality (and during wartime) were determined by clothing. Since the zoot suit was regarded as the badge of delinquency, this signifier alone would expose the wearer to the possibility of assault. One twelve-year-old *pachuco* casualty expressed his incomprehension of hostility to the suit from his hospital bed: 'So our guys wear tight bottoms on their pants and those bums wear wide bottoms. Who the hell are they fighting, Japs or us?'[25]

The roots of the zoot suit show just how ironic the style of the *pachucos* was in its playing with traditional gentlemanly styles but flouting the traditions invested in them. The *New York Times* reported the first purchase of a zoot suit to have been in Gainesville, Georgia. The buyer was a young black man named Clyde Duncan who had been inspired by the Civil War uniform worn by Rhett Butler in the film *Gone With The Wind*: the long frock coat and the baggy trousers.[26] The Yankee soldier is one of the greats in the pageant of North American heroes. By copying this style, the *pachucos* were adopting an ironic posture. They signified their defiance of convention with a style of excessive gentility. The 'badge of delinquency' that the zoot suit was branded with was, in fact, playing with the styles of old-fashioned, sophisticated respectability.

The zoot suit style was literally unpatriotic in that it ignored the exigencies of the wartime climate by contravening fabric rationing regulations. Its cut was generous and used large amounts of fabric. In April 1942, the War Preparedness Board cloth conservation order 'banned pleats, cuffs and long jackets' and legal manufacturers duly stopped making them.[27] The suit continued to be available on the black market. Its extravagance set it up as the subversive, flamboyant Other to the functional service dress of the conscripts who wore short hair and work pants. If service uniform was designed for work, then the zoot suit was designed for the opposite. Its features assured impracticality: the heaviness and formality of the outfit restricted physical activity and served only to be seen in.[28] The zoot suit was overtly Hispanicised with ethnic markers such as crucifixes and patron saint medallions, and Catholic iconic tattoos, of which the Virgin of Guadalupe, the patron Virgin of Mexico, was a favourite.

In his work, *The Labyrinth of Solitude*, the Mexican Noble Laureate Octavio Paz dedicates a chapter to the zoot suit as a unique form of cultural display. The essay entitled 'The Pachuco and Other Extremes' examines *pachuquismo* as the logical extension of the precarious position occupied by Mexicans living in Los Angeles, reflecting 'a psychic oscillation between two irreducible worlds – the North American and the Mexican'. Paz perceives the *pachucos'* strategies of rebellion as typically Mexican. The act of dressing up, of putting on a mask, stems from a long-standing Mexican tradition of using clothes to satirise.[29] The *pachucos* cultivate the disguise that Mexicans feel they are obliged to wear just to survive in LA. The disguise is not to distract attention but rather to attract it, defiantly flaunting their differences to a culture that refuses to countenance them. According to Paz: 'the purpose of [the *pachuco*'s] grotesque dandyism and anarchic behaviour is not so much to point out the injustice and incapacity of a society that has failed to assimilate him as it is to demonstrate his personal will to remain different'.[30] The zoot suit is a proud assertion of difference, and yet its unacceptability invites attack. The zoot suiter courts disaster by making himself into what Paz terms 'the hunter's prey', decking himself out for the chase. Persecution is what completes the *pachuco*'s performance. It is a display that courts hostile attention.

The *pachucos*' identity was based on performance, on the assumption of an identity rather than the bearing of one already inherited. They were the first of the Mexican-American community to formulate an identity as public figures that was contrary to the mainstream but also separate from their inherited identity as Mexicans. The word 'Chicano', a politicised term of self-definition for the American of Mexican descent, has its roots in *Caló*, the *pachuco* language.[31] The *pachuco* legacy of style and attitude reached deep into *barrio* culture and was maintained by the *cholos*

– the Hispanic low riders of the 1960s – and subsequently the *vatos locos* – homeboys of the modern-day gangs.

The zoot suit, as a revolutionary act of cultural display, played an important role in the history of the Chicano civil rights movement. As the first people to position themselves in opposition to the North American mainstream and their marginal Mexican backgrounds, the *pachucos* served as an inspiration for white youths during the Cold War of the 1950s and then student activists. Their language and dress were to be emulated, the writer Carlos Muñoz Jr remembers, and their code of *carnalismo* – absolute love within Chicano gangs – was to be the central concept in the developing ideology of the movement.[32]

The zoot suit was an act of cultural articulation years before the cultural renaissance of the Chicano civil rights movement. As seminal as some of the founding texts, it moved the culture forward in its performance of a unique ethnic identity. As a display of un-Americanism, the zoot suit became a marker of ethnic and racial pride. The suit surfaces as a motif in much Chicano cultural production. Judith Baca's mural, the *Great Wall of Los Angeles*, dedicates a section to the Zoot Suit Riots. Its depiction of the events of June 1943 focuses on the role that clothing played in establishing the dynamics of the riots. The *pachuco* is presented half-naked, stripped of his offending clothing and in a position suggestive both of downtrodden victim-hood and of coiled force ready to be released. The jackboots in the foreground, obvious symbols of fascism, collude with the characteristic flared trouser bottoms of the naval uniform, above which a pair of hands hold the trophy of the drape jacket.[33] The service uniforms provide a frame of normality within which the *pachuco*, the transgressor of these authorised style codes, is presented. The artist presents each item of clothing as loaded with meaning, and the unacceptable subversiveness of the suit is heightened by its partial absence.

The potent roots of the 1950s youth look, however, were eventually watered down. Karal Ann Marling argues that the turning point in Elvis' career was his enlisting in the army. The army barber's clipping away of his *pachuco* ducktail signified the beginning of the end.[34] Just as the Zoot Suit Riots were regarded as a conflict between two styles, so Elvis' *pachuco* flair lost out to military conformity. Quite literally, the army clipped his wings. By the 1960s, the symbolic significance of the zoot suit had disappeared almost completely. It was no longer the fashion in the *barrio*, and it had been replaced by dickies (khaki work trousers), pendeltons (checked shirts) and stocking caps, all evocative of the 1950s style. By the 1970s, the style signified nothing more subversive than youthful rebellion as depicted in the film *Grease*, one that is contained neatly within the structures of respectability as all are handed their highschool diplomas in the last scene of the film.[35] The badge of delinquency that the zoot suit was once branded was served up nostalgically in the 1970s as a harmless style of 1950s teenage rebellion, divested of any specific ethnicity or any real threat to authority. The rebellious style of *Grease* is presented in a framework where it is indulged rather than outlawed as the zoot suit was by the LA authorities.

To wear the zoot suit had once been effectively to criminalise oneself. During the Cold War of the 1950s, it was a display of white teenage rebellion to the prevailing culture of containment. It was the form of clothing that the British designer Vivienne Westwood, termed 'confrontation dressing': wearing clothes that invite critique and hostility, and wearing those styles with pride. It had been a means of asserting a difference, drawing together markers of Yankeeness and Mexicaness and serving them up in a extreme and unnerving form of dandyness. The style set up a masculinity in opposition to the Yankee ideal of manhood. Whilst rebellion and resistance are ends sought by various marginal groups, their means of achieving them are different. The zoot suit is unique in its articulation of cultural difference through style. It is a site inscribed with cultural meanings, making the garment a valuable object of study. That the roots of the zoot suit are Hispanic is a vital factor, given its pervasive influence in the 1950s. Nadel warns against the tendency to assume that the culture of the Cold War was 'for all significant purposes, white'. The zoot suit is emblematic of Hispanic culture's influence upon mainstream 1950s America. It is an influence that is profound and ought not to be underestimated or overlooked.

Notes

1. Richard Martin, 'Style from Paris, Reality from America: Fashion in *Life* Magazine, 1947–1963', *Journal of American Culture*, 19:4 (Winter 1996): 51–5.
2. Stuart Cosgrove, 'The Zoot Suit and Style Warfare', in Angela McRobbie (ed.), *Zoot Suits and Second Hand Dresses* (Basingstoke, UK, Macmillan, 1989), p.5.
3. George Lipsitz, *Time Passages: Collective Memory and American Popular Culture* (Minneapolis, University of Minnesota Press, 1990), p.120.
4. Ibid., pp. 262–3.
5. Ibid., pp. 120–21.
6. Karal Ann Marling, *As Seen on TV* (Cambridge, USA, Harvard University Press, 1994, pp. 169–70.
7. Dick Hebdige, 'Subculture: The Meaning of Style', in Ken Gelder and Sarah Thornton (eds.), *The Subcultures Reader* (London, Routledge, 1997), p. 134.
8. The zoot suit had such power that it was iconised in the 1960s by the Chicano Civil Rights Movement and was upheld as a marker of ethnic pride.
9. 'Youth Gangs Leading Cause of Delinquencies', *Los Angeles Times* (2 June 1943), quoted in Elliot J. Gorn *et al.*, *Constructing the American Past*, vol. 2 (London, HarperCollins, 1995), p. 257.
10. The Sleepy Lagoon Case in which twelve Mexican-American youths were convicted on varying murder charges for the death of José Díaz set the tone for the LAPD's attitude toward Mexican-American youth. The appeal court reversed the lower court's decision two years later, claiming that the evidence was insufficient and had been obtained under prejudiced circumstances. See Gorn *et al.*, *Constructing the American Past*, p.253.
11. Captain Ed Durán Ayres of the Foreign Relations Bureau of Los Angeles Police Department, quoted in Ricardo Romo, *East Los Angeles: History of a Barrio* (Austin, University of Texas Press, 1983), p. 166.
12. Stuart Cosgrove, 'The Zoot Suit and Style Warfare', in Angela McRobbie (ed.), *Zoot Suits and Second Hand Dresses* (Basingstoke, UK, Macmillan, 1989), p. 9.
13. This was the sentiment of the *Mexican Voice* editorial, a newsletter that grew out of the YMCA Mexican Youth Conferences who criticised the *pachucos* for joining in with the Zoot Suit Riots, quoted in Carlos Muñoz Jr, *Youth, Identity,*

Power, (New York, Verso, 1989), p. 38.

14. The words of Manuel de La Raza, pen name of Felix Gutierrez, leader of the Mexican-American Movement, from the *Mexican Voice* (Spring 1942), quoted in Muñoz Jr, *Youth, Identity, Power*, p.39.
15. Cosgrove, 'The Zoot Suit and Style Warfare', p.7.
16. Mauricio Mazón, *The Zoot Suit Riots* (Austin, University of Texas Press, 1984), p.3.
17. Raegan Kelly, 'Hip Hop Chicano' in Brian Cross, *It's not about a Salary ... Rap, Race and Resistance in Los Angeles* (London, Verso, 1993).
18. Eyewitness account of Josephine Fierro de Bright, quoted in Gorn *et al.*, *Constructing the American Past*, p. 255. See also Lipsitz, *Time Passages*, pp. 138–9.
19. 'Zoot Suit War', *Time* (21 June 1943), quoted in Gorn *et al. Constructing the American Past*, p. 271.
20. *Los Angeles Times* (9 June 1943), quoted in Gorn *et al. Constructing the American Past*, p. 258.
21. *New York Times* (7 June 1943), quoted in Gorn *et al. Constructing the American Past*, p. 259.
22. Quoted in 'Zoot Suit War', *Time* (21 June 1943), quoted in Gorn *et al. Constructing the American Past*, p. 271.
23. *New York Times* (7 June 1943), quoted in Gorn *et al.*, *Constructing the American Past*, p. 259.
24. *Examiner* editorial, quoted in 'Zoot Suit War', *Time* (21 June 1943), quoted in Gorn *et al. Constructing the American Past*, p. 271.
25. Ibid. p. 270. The young *pachuco*'s statement is ironic in that those people who straddled the us–them divide, namely Japanese-Americans, had been incarcerated in internment camps since 1942. In other words, the war was being fought not only overseas but also very keenly in America's own backyard against anyone who displayed any traces of un-Americanism.
26. Meyer Berger, 'Zoot Suit Originated in Georgia; Bus Boy Ordered First One in '40', *New York Times* (11 June 1943), quoted in Gorn *et al.*, *Constructing the American Past*, p.264. Malcolm X recalled wearing his zoot suit in Harlem in the 1930s and 1940s: 'I took three of those twenty-five-cent sepia-toned, while-you-wait pictures of myself, posed the way 'hipsters' wearing their zoots would "cool it" – had dangled, knees drawn close together, feet wide apart, both index fingers

jabbed toward the floor. The long coat and the swing chain and the Punjab pants were much more dramatic if you stood that way.' Malcolm X (with Alex Haley), *The Autobiography of Malcolm X* (New York, Grove Press, 1965), pp. 51–2. I am grateful to Andrew Ross for pointing this out to me. See Andrew Ross, *No Respect: Intellectuals and Popular Culture* (New York and London, Routledge, 1989), pp. 82–3.

27. Ross, *No Respect: Intellectuals and Popular Culture*, pp.82–3.
28. Octavio Paz, *The Labyrinth of Solitude*, (London, Penguin, 1985), p. 7.
29. The Day of the Dead in Mexico sees parades in which people dress up in drag or as caricatures of local dignitaries.
30. Paz, *The Labyrinth of Solitude*, p. 9.
31. Film director Luis Valdez first learned the word *Chicano* from his cousin, the zoot suiter Billy Miranda. See Cosgrove, 'The Zoot Suit and Style Warfare', p. 19.
32. Raegan Kelly, 'Hip Hop Chicano'.
33. The viewer's presence is incorporated visually into the mural by the shadow thrown over the *pachuco* in the foreground. The viewer assumes the position of aggressor and is consequently involved in the responsibility for the violence. It is an unsettling mural and one that levels an attack against the whole of the city for its collective responsibility in the victimisation of *pachucos*.
34. Raegan Kelly, 'Hip Hop Chicano', p. 166.
35. Pointing to the film *Grease*, the film-maker Luis Valdez (one of the main figures in the Chicano Cultural Renaissance, and director of the film *Zoot Suit*) believes that the *pachuco* has contributed to the cultural life of America in ways that have not been recognised. The style of the film is clearly that of the *pachuco* and as sported by the T-birds it has implications of ethnic otherness. The film's title encapsulates the dandyish cultivation of coolness with the use of a specific hair product. This is clearly an evocation of the zoot suit style and its foppish masculinity. The film ends with the lovers Sandy and Danny making concessions to each others' styles. Danny dons a jock's jacket but when Sandy turns up in *pachuco* gear, there is no question of which style will win.

CHAPTER FIVE

Mother's Old-Fashioned Gefilte Fish

Nathan Abrams

I wanted out, to be a good American again, kosher again.
Arthur Miller[1]

Jell-O itself both marked and crossed the borderline between Jewish and Christian, American and foreign, kosher and trafe
Marjorie Garber[2]

While the 1950s in the USA have been examined from the perspectives of gender, sexuality, literature, film, theme parks and foreign policy, relatively little has been written about the place of ethnic, or more precisely, Jewish food in 1950s America. There have been general surveys of food and eating in America, including those by Sylvia Lovegren,[3] Harvey Levenstein[4] and Richard J. Hooker.[5] To these, we can add Karal Ann Marling's more specific look at the 1950s.[6] But none of these studies takes more than a glance at ethnic food patterns in America. On the other hand, those studies that do examine ethnic food, such as Claudia Roden's *The Book of Jewish Food*,[7] Jennie Grossinger's *The Art of Jewish Cooking*,[8] and Joan Nathan's *Jewish Cooking in America*,[9] do not focus on the 1950s in any detail. The same can be said of the impressive work of Jenna Weissman Joselit,[10] who has mapped Jewish domestic practices from the 1850s up to 1950.[11]

Thus the topic of ethnic foods strangely marks an absence in our understanding of 1950s culture, which is especially interesting given David Reisman's observation of its increasing importance during this period.[12] This chapter examines one community in particular to demonstrate how discourses of containment, loyalty and America were produced, consumed and negotiated in 1950s America. In the words of the sociologist Herbert Gans: 'Food, we know, plays a significant role in Jewish society, recreational, and religious life in America.'[13] Taking as a starting point Marjorie Garber's essay 'Jell-O', which appeared in the recent collection, *Secret Agents*,[14] this chapter aims to examine the cultural values attached to specific food products at a precise moment in American history of the 1950s, and to explore how these were reconciled with concepts of Jewishness.

JELL-O

On 20 June 1953, Julius and Ethel Rosenberg were executed for the crime of espionage. They had been tried and found guilty of passing atomic secrets to the Soviet Union. The key piece of evidence in the conviction of the Rosenbergs was a box of Jell-O. The prosecution argued that a Jell-O packet was cut in half and used as a password between Julius Rosenberg and Ruth Greenglass. In their detailed study of the case, Ronald Radosh and Joyce Milton describe the alleged scene:

> Later, after the kitchen table had been cleared, Julius asked Ruth to step into the kitchen so that he could give her a recognition signal, to be used in case another courier had to take Ann's place. Julius took a Jell-O box from the kitchen cabinet, removed the contents, and cut the side panel of the box into two irregularly shaped pieces. One he kept, the other he gave to Ruth, who took it into the living room to show her husband. David would later testify that he remarked on what a clever idea the Jell-O box was and Julius, obviously pleased, replied, 'The simplest things are the cleverest.'[15]

The presiding, judge, Irving Kaufman, stated to the jury: 'The Government contends that you have a right to infer that there existed a link between Julius Rosenberg and Yakovlev [the Soviet agent] in that Julius Rosenberg in some way transmitted … the Jell-

O box-side to Yakovlev.'[16] Roy Cohn even went out and bought a box of Jell-O to show to the jury in order to strengthen the government's case. It worked.

To the jury in the Rosenberg case, Jell-O signified guilt. To American Jews it signified *trayf* – a non-kosher food product forbidden for consumption by halachic law. The word derives from the Hebrew for 'torn'.[17] *Trayf* is the opposite of 'kosher', which is one of Judaism's contributions to an international language denoting that which is proper and meets accepted rules and standards. In Judaism, 'kosher' does not refer only to acceptable food. Tefillin (phylacteries) and Torah scrolls are kosher, in that they meet all halachic (Jewish legal) requirements. The expression is also applied to individuals: acceptable witnesses are called *edim k'sherim*; an upright, proper observant Torah Jew is referred to as an *adam kasher* (kosher man).

Jell-O was *trayf* because it contained the ingredient gelatine. Gelatine is derived from the skin and bones of non-kosher animals, in particular pigs, hence it is a prohibited substance. The 1936 *Kosher Food Guide* included an entry entitled 'Jell-O – is it Kosher or Trefa?', which stated:

> Jell-O was absolutely trefa as the gelatine contained in the product is derived from trefa bones and parts of skins, as for instance the skins of hams, etc. As there is unfortunately no kosher animal gelatine produced, we naturally answered to various enquiries about the permissibility of Jell-O or similar products for consumption by Jews that these articles are trefa.[18]

Until certified *pareve* kosher synthetic gelatines came on the market, orthodox Jews would not use any gelatine or Jell-O in their cooking.[19]

Among non-orthodox American Jews, however, it was probably Jell-O's very non-kosherness that made it so enticing. Its packets proudly proclaimed its *trayf*-ness, stating clearly 'Jell-O Brand, Gelatin dessert'. Added to this was its Americanness. Jell-O was a quintessentially *American* product that had originated in 1897.[20] When it appeared in the 1920s and 1930s, it caused a stir within the Jewish community. As Joan Nathan wrote:

> What American in the 1920s and '30s could resist the appetizing photographs of gently rippling Jell-O salads in the *Ladies Home Journal*? The majority of Jews, wanting to embrace everything American, to be part of this new age of science and technology, were open to new products that would shorten their time in the kitchen and these included the new Jell-O deserts.[21]

Jell-O was advertised in Jewish publications and eaten in Jewish homes; its popularity amongst Jews was undeniable. Indeed, once Julius had removed the contents of the Jell-O box, Ethel undoubtedly used them to make the dessert. Recipes for Jell-O desserts began to appear in Jewish cookbooks. From the 1930s to the 1950s, therefore, despite a certain amount of consternation amongst orthodox Jews, the majority of non-practising American Jewry considered Jell-O to be safe, 'kosher', and American. This changed as a result of the Rosenberg case. As Garber noted: 'Jell-O itself both marked and crossed the borderline between Jewish and Christian, American and foreign, kosher and *trafe*.'[22] In the paranoid era of the 1950s, the differences between kosher and *trayf* marked the boundaries between loyalty and subversion, pro-American and Communist.

The Rosenbergs were convicted by a box of Jell-O, thus Jell-O became a sign of guilt. Since the Rosenbergs were guilty of passing atomic secrets to the Soviet Union, Jell-O became a signifier for subversion, disloyalty and un-American activity. What is more, because Jell-O was un-kosher, these labels became subsumed under the umbrella term, *trayf*. As a result, these practices were then marked as un-Jewish. Leo Rosten's *The Joys of Yiddish* describes a *trayf* person as 'someone untrustworthy, malicious, tricky, of whom you should be aware'.[23]

MOTHERHOOD

A common stereotype amongst Jews is that of the Jewish mother figure. This stereotype constructs the Jewish mother as an over-caring matriarchal figure who stuffs her children with far more than they can possibly digest. A key strand of the prosecution's case against the Rosenbergs was the denigration of Ethel as a bad mother. Ethel and Julius's son, Robert, observed: 'It was particularly important to cast my parents in a bad light, because the public might otherwise come to feel sympathy for a young married couple with small children and recoil at the government's act of killing them.'[24] Thus, the Rosenbergs were demonised as bad parents. In sentencing them to death, Judge Irving Kaufman stated:

> Indeed the defendants Julius and Ethel Rosenberg placed their devotion to their cause above their own personal safety and were conscious that they were sacrificing their own children, should their misdeeds be detected – all of which did not deter them from pursuing their course. Love for their course dominated their lives – it was even greater than their love for their children.[25]

Robert added that he felt Kaufmann 'believed that by sentencing them to death he was doing my brother and me a favor by making sure that we did not grow up in the household'.[26] What is more, he 'sought to absolve himself and the government for orphaning Michael and me by blaming my parents for what happened to us'.[27] The government's chief ally within the American-Jewish community, the American Jewish Committee (AJC), was also very concerned with the status of the Rosenberg boys, devoting a great deal of energy to ensuring that they were not used as the focus of an anti-American, pro-Rosenberg propaganda campaign. A prominent attorney and member of the AJC, Morris Ernst, for example, volunteered to offer his analysis of the dynamics of the Rosenbergs' relationship to the FBI as well as to become the Rosenbergs' attorney so that he could assist the FBI better.

Ethel, in particular, was personally targeted. She was characterised as the dominant partner in the marriage. In sentencing them, Judge Kaufman described Ethel as the 'prime mover'.[28] Ernst observed that: 'Julius is the slave and his wife, Ethel, is the master.'[29] President Eisenhower, in his wisdom, felt that 'in this instance it is the woman who is the strong and recalcitrant character, the man is the weak one. She has obviously been the leader in everything they did in the spy ring.'[30] These images were picked up and conveyed by the press. In contrast to the *baleboosteh*, which stood for a praiseworthy mother, Ethel was presented as a poor mother to her children. Her refusal to break down under the pressure of her arrest and trial was taken as evidence that she lacked maternal feeling, that she cared more for Communism than for her own children. She was variously described as 'cold', 'lacking "normal" feminine characteristics', 'unnatural' and 'steely, stony, tight-lipped'. One juror explained, 'I had two daughters at the time, and it bothered me how they would subject their children to such a thing. I just couldn't understand it.'[31] One FBI report stated that 'Ethel was not a good mother after all.'[32] Ethel was publicly demonised as 'silent and mysterious, conspiratorial and political, dominating and evil'.[33]

These characterisations of the Rosenbergs were propagated among elements of the Jewish community. The AJC was keen to distance American Jewry from the Rosenbergs. Hence it co-operated in the fashioning of Julius and Ethel as a dysfunctional family in contrast to the tight-knit family units that were so important to Judaism. It even collaborated with the State Department to produce a book to this end.[34] Ethel stood in opposition to the stereotype of the Jewish mother that they were so keen to uphold. Good Jewish mothers did not abandon their children for secular, atheist causes; good Jewish mothers fed their children wholesome Jewish, kosher cooking – not Jell-O. Ethel was a bad Jewish mother not only because she fed her children un-kosher, *trayf* food products, but because she neglected them for a secular, atheistic ideology.

The AJC set up counter-products to Jell-O. Through its magazine, *Commentary*, the AJC promoted a Jewish cuisine that was ethnically sound (kosher) but at the same time loyal and American. *Commentary* was established by the AJC in 1945 as 'a journal of significant thought and opinion on Jewish affairs and contemporary issues'. The magazine had no religious affiliation and hence did not promote any particular sectarian agenda. Many of its writers took a secular, liberal, anti-Communist view to most subjects. Its editorial board was composed of ex-radicals who had abandoned Trotskyism in the 1930s and 1940s. The AJC, for most of its early existence, was drawn from the wealthy middle- and upper-middle-class German Jews, who had immigrated to America during the last century. *Commentary*'s editors, on the other hand, represented the poorer Eastern European Jews who had emigrated at the turn of this century. Nonetheless they sought to produce a journal of highbrow thought that distinguished itself from both the masses and the more mediocre elements of the middle-class American Jewry. Food played a part in this process.

Commentary did not advertise Jell-O products. Jell-O was ersatz: it benefited from the huge increase in newly developed and sophisticated flavourings and food colourings during the 1950s, which led to a concomitant decrease in reliance on natural fruit and flavours. In defence of this, a General Foods researcher claimed: 'There are not sufficient strawberries grown in the world to supply the demand for strawberry flavor.'[35] It was mass-produced and hence commodified. It was linked to the Rosenbergs and thus subversive, disloyal and Communistic. Jell-O represented the worst excesses of Stalinism. Reading the pages of *Commentary* and the writings of those who contributed to it elsewhere, a clear distaste for mass culture can be discerned. Mass culture was linked to Stalinism and the Popular Front period of history, of which the Rosenbergs were the paradigm. Through the Rosenbergs, Jell-O came to symbolise the middlebrow, mass-commodified culture of the Popular Front era. Thus, its excision from the pages of *Commentary* stood for an attempt to circumscribe that culture and write it out of the history of American Jewry.

Instead of Jell-O, *Commentary* advertised traditionally Jewish food products. These were represented as being quintessentially authentic foods that contained real and natural ingredients, unlike the ersatz and *trayf* Jell-O. Perhaps the most prominent was Mother's Old-Fashioned Gefilte Fish. Gefilte fish means 'stuffed fish'. It is basically a poached fish-ball made from whitefish, pike or carp with filler (bread crumbs or matzah meal) served on the Sabbath and holy days among German and Eastern European Jews. Gefilte fish carried the mark of Jewish authenticity. *The Jewish Home Beautiful*, the guide for aspiring Jewish mothers, stated: 'If there is any one particular food that might lay claim to being the

Figure 1: Advertisement for Mother's Old-Fashioned Gelfilite Fish. (This advert originally appeared in *Commentary*, 22:3 (September 1956), p. 289, and *Commentary*, 23:4 (April 1957), p. 397.

Jewish national dish, gefilte fish is that food.'[36] Mother's advertised their product by connecting it to history and tradition (Figure 1). It is 'old-fashioned', unlike the newly developed Jell-O. It is the 'real' thing (underlined for emphasis), unlike the ersatz Jell-O. It is made in the 'finest tradition' and carries with it all of the symbols of kashrut and Jewish authenticity, including Hebrew writing. Had Ethel read her *Jewish Home Beautiful*, she would have learned that the good Jewish mother serves her children gefilte fish (hence 'homestyle') and should not be filling them with *trayf* products. In contrast to Ethel stand 'one million' Jewish mothers who know better. One million Jewish mothers are not subversive or disloyal. They are loyal Americans who give their kids loyal, kosher foods.

Gefilte fish took its place as the centrepiece of Jewish cooking. The importance of gefilte fish to Jewish cuisine was demonstrated in September 1954, which marked the tercentenary of the arrival of Jews in America. Banquets were held to mark the event as an important date in Jewish-American memory. The most important of these banquets was the National Tercentenary Dinner held on 20 October in New York City, at which President Eisenhower was the guest of honour. It was considered that gefilte fish was good enough even for the president.[37] On the more everyday level, ready-made gefilte fish entered Jewish food consciousness to such an extent that by the 1970s, a jar of Manischewitz gefilte fish was essential to celebrating Jewish holy days.[38] During the 1950s, gefilte fish was further popularised for a mass audience by *The Goldbergs*, an immensely popular television programme that attracted some 40 million viewers per week. The eponymous heroine of the show, Molly Goldberg, was invited by a leading food manufacturer to produce some of her own recipe gefilte fish in his test kitchen.[39] Thus, as Donald Weber has pointed out, ethnic food became an 'agent of social incorporation: how, that is, the offering of (say) gefilte fish enacts a ritual of integration, of conformity, above all of reassurance.'[40]

Other adverts include those for Manischewitz and Streit's matzot (Figure 2), as well as Pepsi-Cola. To link these foods produced under the most modern conditions ('inner-wrapped') with their heritage, traditional Jewish symbols were invoked such as the menorah and Hebrew lettering. Pepsi-Cola, another quintessentially American product, was reinvented to connect Americanness (loyalty) with tradition as it also obtained the ritual seal of approval during the 1950s. Pepsi, Manischewitz matzah and gefilte fish were all linked by what Jell-O is not: the symbols of kashrut (the *hechsher*). Jell-O can never be kosher because it contains gelatine – to remove it would irrevocably alter the product. These other products, however, were kosher, safe and loyal. When that juror could not understand 'how they would subject their children to such a thing', that 'thing' was Jell-O.

The need to authenticate certain products as traditional and kosher became more imperative in this era as food technology

Figure 2: Advertisement for Manischewitz matzot. (Printed by permission of The B. Manischewitz Company.)

improved. The 1950s witnessed the age of processed food and TV dinners, backed up by bold, colourful adverts that proclaimed their benefits. Kashrut came under further threat from the opening of the first McDonalds restaurant in 1954, the establishment of the McDonalds corporation the following year, and the advent of standardised production-line hamburgers. What is more, suburbanisation and a move away from the observance of previous generations increasingly threatened traditional Jewish practices. In his famous study of a Jewish suburban community, Marshall Sklare observed a decline in maintaining kosher homes.[41] While approximately 46 per cent of an earlier generation had bought kosher meat, surveys of their children estimated that only five to ten per cent continued to do so.[42] The sensitivity surrounding kosher food at this time was demonstrated by the uproar caused by Isaac Rosenfeld's Freudian interpretation of the kashrut laws that appeared in *Commentary* in 1949.[43] Rosenfeld suggested that the dietary laws echoed the injunctions in sexual behaviour and that the desire to eat *trayf* mirrored the urge to participate in the world of forbidden sexuality. It was the only article that *Commentary*'s editor, Elliot Cohen, ever publicly apologised for publishing.

To counteract these trends, or to exploit a niche in the market, manufacturers began a twin process of mass production of traditional

Jewish foods and the 'kosherisation' of American products. Matzot, gefilte fish and borscht all became available in prepared form. This had the effect of promoting the celebration of Jewish life while decreasing the time and energy expended in such celebrations. Pepsi-Cola, Maxwell House coffee, jam, soups, sweets, cakes, noodles, ketchup and hundreds of other products were sanctioned for use in kosher homes and on holidays, thus enabling Jews to celebrate their festivals with American products. Joselit remarked, 'Thus almost every American diet staple is now available in kosher or Passover form.'[44] In advertising these products, manufacturers highlighted a commitment to family and domestic life in contrast to the dysfunctional Rosenberg family. Advertising encouraged a desire for these new kosher products, whilst simultaneously diminishing misgivings about packaged, mass-produced foods. Kosher products emerged with the double marking of the traditional rabbinical imprimatur and of modern science's approval. Companies such as Manischewitz and Streit employed the latest techniques to guarantee the utmost hygiene and freshness.[45]

Joselit believes that 'it is not too far-fetched to say that these advertisements, together with the food products themselves, became new, typically twentieth century resources in the preservation and affirmation of Jewish identity.'[46] Marshall McLuhan observed that 'any acceptable ad is a vigorous dramatization of communal experience'.[47] And Jackson Lears pointed out how advertising folk icons such as Aunt Jemima, Aunt Belle, Betty Crocker and, in this case, the Jewish Mother 'epitomized a whole constellation of nuturant values associated with the preindustrial household and community life' for an uprooted suburban bourgeoisie that felt unconnected with their communities of origin.[48] 'Traditional foods and ways of eating,' it has been stated, 'form a link with the past and help ease the shock of entering a new culture.'[49] As a consequence 'the consumption of kosher foods became a way of affirming and celebrating tradition, Jewish identity, and cultural continuity'.[50] A new category of Jewishness emerged – the 'gastronomic Jew', who derived his or her identity from digestion of ethnic foodstuffs rather than from scrupulous observance of the dietary laws.[51] Nathan Glazer and William H. Whyte both noted a 'Jewish revival' and 'a revival among Jews of religious and cultural practices which intensify one's sense of Jewishness ... such as the dietary laws'.[52] Kashrut suddenly enjoyed a new popularity in post-war American-Jewish life, leading Ruth Glazer to write that 'the egg beater is today the most effective weapon for propagating the faith'.[53] New cookbooks were produced in the 1950s to meet and encourage the 'kosher revival': *The Molly Goldberg Cookbook*, *The Art of Jewish Cooking*, *The Jewish Holidays and Their Favorite Foods*, *The Jewish Holiday Cookbook*, and *Aunt Fanny's Junior Jewish Cookbook.*

Through food, American Jews in the 1950s attempted to move into the American mainstream, but on their own terms. They sought to articulate their loyalty to America (kosher) while simultaneously distancing themselves from subversive elements such as the Rosenbergs (*trayf*). Through food, this was achieved by the promotion of traditional Jewish products that fitted into the American way of life, as well as the incorporation of American products into the traditional Jewish way of life. The history of American Jews in the 1950s, therefore, demonstrates Donna R. Gabaccia's observation of 'the symbolic power of food to reflect cultural or social affinities in moments of change or transformation'.[54]

Notes

1. Arthur Miller, 'After the Fall', in Arthur Miller, *Plays: Two*, p. 184.
2. Marjorie Garber, 'Jello', in Marjorie Garber and Rebecca L. Walkowitz (eds.), *Secret Agents: The Rosenberg Case, McCarthyism, and Fifties America* (New York and London, Routledge, 1995), p. 21. Please note that since the word 'trafe' is a transliterated term, its spelling differs between sources. Where possible, I have used the spelling 'trayf'.
3. Sylvia Lovegren, *Fashionable Food: Seven Decades of Food Fads* (New York, Simon & Schuster, 1995).
4. Harvey Levenstein, *Paradox of Plenty: A Social History of Eating in Modern America* (Oxford, Oxford University Press, 1988).
5. Richard J. Hooker, *Food and Drink in America: A History* (New York, The Bobbs-Merrill Co., Inc., 1981).

6. Karal Ann Marling, *As Seen on TV: The Visual Culture of Everyday Life in the 1950s* (Cambridge, USA, Harvard University Press, 1994).
7. Claudia Roden, *The Book of Jewish Food* (London, Viking, 1997).
8. Jennie Grossinger, *The Art of Jewish Cooking* (New York, Random House, 1958).
9. Joan Nathan, *Jewish Cooking in America* (New York, Alfred A. Knopf, 1995).
10. Jenna Weissman Joselit, '"A Set Table": Jewish Domestic Culture in the New World', in Susan L. Braunstein and Jenna Weissman Joselit (eds), *Getting Comfortable in New York: The American Jewish Home, 1890–1950* (New York, The Jewish Museum, 1990), pp. 19-73.
11. Jenna Weissman Joselit, 'Jewish in Dishes: Kashrut in the New World', in Robert M. Seltzer and Norman J. Cohen (eds) *The Americanization of the Jews* (New York and London, New York University Press, 1995), pp. 247–64; and Jenna Weissman Joselit, *The Wonders of America: Reinventing Jewish Culture 1880–1950* (New York, Hill & Wang, 1995).
12. David Reisman, Nathan Glazer and Reuel Denney, *The Lonely Crowd: A Study of the Changing American Character*, abridged edn (New York, Doubleday Anchor Books, 1953), p. 171.
13. Herbert J. Gans, 'American Jewry: Present and Future', *Commentary*, 21 (May 1956), p. 428.
14. Garber, 'Jell-O', pp. 11–22.
15. Ronald Radosh and Joyce Milton, *The Rosenberg File* (New Haven and London, Yale University Press, 1997), p. 69.
16. Quoted in Garber, 'Jell-O', p. 11.
17. Leo Rosten, *The Joys of Yiddish* (London, Penguin, 1968), p. 417.
18. Quoted in Nathan, *Jewish Cooking in America*, p. 364.
19. Ibid.
20. For a concise history of a centenary of Jell-O, see the official Jell-O website, www.kraftfoods.com/jell-o/history/.
21. Nathan, *Jewish Cooking in America*, p. 364.
22. Garber, 'Jell-O', p. 21.
23. Rosten, *The Joys of Yiddish*, p. 417.
24. Robert Meeropol, 'Rosenberg Realities', in Marjorie Garber and Rebecca L. Walkowitz (eds), *Secret Agents: The Rosenberg Case, McCarthyism, and Fifties America* (New York and London, Routledge, 1995), p. 239.
25. Ibid. p. 240.
26. Ibid.

27. Ibid.
28. Quoted in Radosh and Milton, *The Rosenberg File*, p. 284.
29. Quoted in Meeropol, 'Rosenberg Realities', p. 240.
30. Ibid.
31. Quoted in Joyce Antler, 'A Bond of Sisterhood: Ethel Rosenberg, Molly Goldberg, and Radical Jewish Women of the 1950s', in Marjorie Garber and Rebecca L. Walkowitz (eds), *Secret Agents: The Rosenberg Case, McCarthyism, and Fifties America* (New York and London, Routledge, 1995), p. 206.
32. Ibid.
33. Ibid. p. 207.
34. Solomon Andhil Fineberg, *The Rosenberg Case: Fact and Fiction* (New York, Oceana, 1953).
35. Quoted in Harvey Levenstein, *Paradox of Plenty: A Social History of Eating in Modern America* (New York and Oxford, Oxford University Press, 1993), p. 109.
36. Betty D. Greenberg and Anthea O. Silverman, *The Jewish Home Beautiful*, 9th edn (New York, The National Women's League of the United Synagogue of America, 1958), p. 126.
37. *New York Times* (21 October 1954), quoted from Edward S. Shapiro, *A Time for Healing: American Jewry since World War II* (Baltimore and London, The Johns Hopkins University Press, 1992), p. 92.
38. See, for example, the recollection of Susan Gubar in 'Eating the Bread of Affliction: Judaism and Feminist Criticism', in Jeffrey Rubin-Dorsky and Shelley Fisher Fishkin (eds), *People of the Book: Thirty Scholars Reflect on Their Jewish Identity.* (Madison, The University of Wisconsin Press, 1996), p. 16.
39. The episode was entitled 'Molly's Fish'. I am grateful to Jena Weissman Joselit for pointing this out in her *The Wonders of America*, p. 197. For more detail on this episode, see Donald Weber, 'Memory and Repression in Early Ethnic Television: The Example of Gertrude Berg and *The Goldbergs*', in *The Other Fifties: Interrogating Midcentury American Icons* (Urbana and Chicago, Univeristy of Illinois Press, 1997), 159–61.
40. Weber, 'Memory and Repression in Early Ethnic Television', p. 158.
41. Marshall Sklare, *Conservative Judaism: An American Religious Movement* (New York, Schocken Books, 1972), p. 204.
42. Joselit, '"A Set Table"', p. 59.
43. Isaac Rosenfeld, 'Adam and Eve on Delancey Street', *Commentary*, 8 (October 1949), pp. 385–7.

44. Joselit, *The Wonders of America*, pp. 195–7.
45. Ibid., p. 188.
46. Joselit, '"A Set Table"', p. 57.
47. Marshall McLuhan, *Understanding Media: The Extensions of Man* (London, Abacus, 1974), p. 243.
48. T.J. Jackson Lears, *Fables of Abundance: A Cultural History of Advertising in America* (New York, Basic Books, 1994), p. 348.
49. Susan Kalcik, 'Ethnic Foodways in America: Symbol and the Performance of Identity', in L.K. Brown and K. Mussel (eds.), *Ethnic and Regional Foodways in the United States: The Performance of Group Identity* (Knoxville, Univesity of Tennessee Press, 1984), p. 37.
50. Joselit, 'Jewish in Dishes', p. 257.
51. Joselit, '"A Set Table"', p. 55.
52. Nathan Glazer, 'The Jewish Revival in America', *Commentary*, 20 (December 1955), p. 493; and William H. Whyte, Jr, *The Organization Man* (New York, Doubleday Anchor Books, 1957), pp. 414–15.
53. Ruth Glazer, 'Holiday Cook', *Commentary*, 21 (March 1956), p. 294.
54. Donna R. Gabaccia, *We Are What We Eat: Ethnic Food and the Making of Americans* (Cambridge, USA, Harvard University Press, 1998), p. 9.

CHAPTER SIX

Not on his wavelength: experiments with radio by John Cage

Ben Andrews

One of the most famous of essays on radio that dates from the Cold War is Theodor Adorno's *A Social Critique of Radio Music*.[1] Adorno considered the effect of electronic transmission on listening to music, given the vast proliferation of mass media forms in the era. Although both Adorno and John Cage shared a disdain for the popular, a myopia revealing their 'high-art' orientation, both figures were concerned with how listening had become seemingly effortless and music pre-packaged in post-war America: 'It is the ideal of Aunt Jemima's ready-mix for pancakes extended to the field of music.'[2]

Despite sharing similar concerns with Adorno about the social use of the radio, John Cage's work in the 1950s provides an insight into the dissemination of broadcast sound unlike that of mass-society criticism that Adorno typified. He allows interesting and unusual links to be made between two major features of Cold War scholarship: the domestic technology of 'everyday life' and the cosmic technology of 'outer space'. To a degree, Cage anticipated the belief in unconventional spiritual concerns in a technological America that were to be made famous by Ken Kesey and Jack Kerouac as the decade progressed. In addition, the style of artistic practice that he began in the 1950s had tremendous influence on the experimental tradition for the next two decades. Such practices disturbed the generic distinction but loosely encompassed ideas of chance, simultaneity and 'performance' ideas that Cage explored in the 1950s. But it is not so much the content as the location or social position in 1950s America that makes Cage's work interesting. Because Cage's avant-garde project is located some distance away from the popular arts of the decade, his work is overlooked by scholars in search of a Cold War Zeitgeist as not 'reflecting' or shedding light upon general changes and attitudes. Even his isolation is taken as symptomatic of a general conformism and conservatism. But although the musical avant-garde was certainly not as fashionable and popular as it was to be in the 1960s, it should be noted that such work was located, if rather problematically, within a specific tradition of musical practice found within metropolitan music schools, conservatories and colleges, particularly around New York City and the East Coast, as it still is. Geographical isolation aside, in the experimental tradition, the characteristic of 'seriousness' or 'difficulty' of the music is precisely one of its purposes, aiming to preserve or create a uniqueness or buffer against 'improper', i.e. commercial, use. A deliberate thwarting of immediate accessibility is part of its project, it attempts not simply to reflect or be reflected in wider society. Crucially, it is necessary to 'unlearn' certain modes of listening that had been promoted by or for commercial use. So, despite rather than because of this relative musical obscurity, Cage's work provides an essential insight into the pattern of containment and apparent conformity. Certain ways of listening entered the domestic environment via the new technology made specifically for this space – the domestic radio set. These were ways of listening that were not only bound up with the machine from which the sounds came – its dials and controls – but also enabled new access and freedoms to the very specific patterns of the global and cosmic order of Cold War America.

Despite his famous maxim from 1959 – 'I have nothing to say and I am saying it and that is poetry as I need it'[3] – there is much to say about John Cage (1912–92), a star figure in the American tradition of dissent. Although originating from the strict modernist concerns of Arnold Schoenberg, a European composer exiled in America by the 1930s, Cage distanced himself from Schoenberg's battles against romantic, over-ripe bombast to create works that assumed very disparate and open forms. His performances were cast with the shadow of his mentors' resilience for experimentation, but they made their modernist polemic seem hermetically sealed from a post-war artistic climate of mixed media and mechanical reproducibility. Schoenberg's intention in the first two decades of the century had been to free music from the classical structures of Western music. He sought to dispense with the tyranny that tonal hierarchies had held over the narrative of a piece of music, governing the choice of notes and keys as it had done for centuries. In trying to start anew, Schoenberg created a sound world in which all notes had an equal value in a chosen series and any set of notes in the scale could be chosen as the important. This series or set acted as a composition's framework. John Cage was the first in the experimental tradition to move one step further. As Schoenberg dispensed with classical determinacy to establish an alternative compositional process, thereby liberating sounds from traditional subservience to a musical narrative, so Cage dispensed with determinacy altogether to relinquish intention over the outcome of the compositional processes, now plural.

Additionally, Cage proceeded musical democratisation, past giving all notes equal value, to work with sounds considered musical and non-musical, seeking to liberate sounds from a tyranny of 'music'. This 'letting the sounds be themselves' involved an eroding of control over the compositional process itself, one's aesthetic judgement and one's control over the resulting performance, characteristics of the Western tradition that Schoenberg's modernism held intact.[4] By emphasising the composition as a *process*, Cage expanded and opened composition, reinvigorating the notion of experimentation as a discovering of what might happen if certain things are tried, as a scientific experiment tries to find out what will happen within certain variables. By using tools of indeterminacy, and by using non-musical sound – strategies that had first arisen in other modernisms of Futurism, Dada and Surrealism – Cage was able to break from the Western tradition of music and music-making.

Crucially, John Cage was able to make this break at the point in his career in which he was able to find a ready-made technological equivalent to his particular philosophy of 'unlearning' traditional modes of listening. He found the equivalent of such thought in 1950s America itself, in the technology and use of the radio set and its recorded sounds. In his pieces of this era radio sets themselves were featured in groups or with the performers on stage, alongside other more traditional instruments; what ever happens to be broadcast was to be 'played' by adjusting the controls. Cage's use of the radio and broadcast sound is of interest not as a medium for communication as such, but as a means to an awareness of the possibilities that could arise from post-war America's electronic environment and the everyday life it had correspondingly transformed.

Even though Cage's work was inflected with his mentor's concern for finding new ways, the newness might best be described as playing on a sense of novelty. They appeared slightly 'gimmicky'. His former pupil, the artist Allan Kaprow, neatly summarised Cage's project: 'Cage made two principal experimental moves in music making: the sustained practice of chance operations to arrange and select sounds and durations of a piece, and the welcoming of noise into a composition as equivalent to conventional musical sound.'[5]

Consider this quotation from Calvin Tomkins' famous essay on John Cage, first published in the *New Yorker* in the early 1960s:

> Cage's teaching method in the music course was to introduce his students to the work he was currently engaged in, and the ideas behind it, and then encourage them to experiment on their own. 'He established this feeling of suspended gentleness right at the start,' said Allan Kaprow, who took the course for two years, 'and most of the people who started out in it just weren't on his wavelength at all, so the class soon narrowed down to seven or eight.'[6]

Most of the students who attended Cage's course on Experimental Music at the New School for Social Research, New York, from the autumn of 1956 found his approach puzzling.[7] Expecting a history of the modernist avant-garde, the enrolled pupils might have found it rather disorienting to find out that they themselves would have to experiment. The story stands as a model for Cageian practice and reception.

Consider also this quotation from the closing paragraphs of John Hollander's 1962 review of Cage's *Silence: lectures and writings*:

> Mr Cage comes off throughout much of *Silence* as a kind of jovial guru. It is obvious that he is terribly serious about music, nostalgic for the cosmological role of music in the mediaeval and Renaissance world-pictures, and terribly willing to use any means at hand, preferably modish, to construct both a new model of musica speculativa and a new model of music to match it. Silence contains within it, in dispersed form, the pattern of this model.[8]

Notice, in the last sentence, the effect the title has in transforming almost any statement about the book into one that might have come from it. Hollander's comments are interesting. The establishment of a 'world-picture' and a 'cosmological role of music' is particularly relevant to Cage's involvement with radio. Cage chose to use shortwave in his compositions, a frequency chosen for its ability to travel great distances around the world connecting antipodean localities. In 1950, ninety million radio sets were in use in the USA – an average of two radios for every home in the country. In 1952, Sony marketed the miniature transistor radio, mainly for government and research, seeing widespread popular use two years later. In 1953, Voice of America enhanced its broadcast to the Soviet Bloc. In 1955 alone, seven million new sets were produced, climbing to eleven million by the beginning of the 1960s. Concomitantly, by 1958, stereo records arrived in high-street stores.[9]

The 1950s were also a time of the first radio telescopes, with Jodrell Bank in England opening in 1957. Radiowaves of a much longer wavelength than light can be detected by sensitive receivers, thereby enabling the study of much more distant and much older cosmological forms. In 1952, workers in Holland, America and Australia detected gaseous hydrogen by this means, discovering that such clouds lie in the spiral arms of galaxies. By 1962, radio-astronomers located a signal strong enough to be photographed, leading to the discovery of quasars – relatively small objects that generate inconceivably great amounts of energy so that they appear bright at huge distances.[10]

So Cage's 'modish' engagement with radio was, in one sense, illustrative of the communications expansion in the decade that he was working in and responding to. The ability of radiowaves to reach minute details in the universe brought to light the previously imperceptible and found patterns there. Accordingly, Cage was interested in the expansion of listening potential into what was once considered an absence, by arguing that there is never such a thing as silence. Furthermore, the sheer amount of domestic and commercial radiowaves around the earth, and the popularisation of the stereo long-playing record, increased the availability of disembodied and mechanically-reproduced sound. This was often music packaged for domestic use in sitting rooms, but increasingly pushed out or turned off by the ascendant television set.

Parallel with the boom in radio production, by 1953 there were 326 television stations broadcasting to a total of twenty-one million US homes.[11] Where once a sitting room centred on a hearth, in modern suburban homes the 'lounge' centred on this series of disembodied images from the communications revolution. The radio, on the other hand, did not demand the degree of attention that the television demanded, the listener not needing to look at the source of sound, especially as it became smaller and more portable with the popularisation of transistors. Sounds became doubly disembodied from their sources. The sounds of a radio symphony orchestra playing in Rockefeller Center, New York City arrived in the nation's living rooms. The sounds from the radio relaying the transmission were de-centred from its position as a hearth to the desired effect of musical, and eventually stereophonic, ambience. Furthermore, as a focus of everyday life, the lounge was a site for the consumption or reception of music.

For Cage, this shift did not necessarily entail a corresponding loss of any unique aura of music in an age of mechanical reproducibility.

What the radio might be said to have produced is an extension of experience, in which everyday life for the millions had been opened up to a globalised culture and transformed by the communications revolution. This line of thought follows Cage's interest in Marshall McLuhan's writings and is one that this chapter will return to later. However, rather than adopting the traditional avant-garde approach towards disseminated music – i.e. that it fosters lazy listening or drowns out well-nurtured sounds – Cage's engagement with the radio is more interesting and nuanced, his distaste for harmony aside: sound had become packaged by technology, and a poverty of listening resulted. Throughout the 1950s, the advent of push-button radios increased radio ownership, starting with an initial sales run of five million in 1951. Listening to the radio became a more ordered and structured experience and Cage's work can be seen as a disruption of this tendency arising from push-button radio to regulate the signal. His work for radio attempted to move away from the mechanised processes of structured and selective listening that the machine began to foster. Listening to his radio pieces, the listener soon realises that one does not simply wait for the sound from the various stations to emerge from amongst the static, but that the distinction between sounds and so-called 'extraneous' noise is not a helpful listening strategy – 'gaps' seem just as aurally interesting.

Apart from playing a role in Cage's attempts to level the hierarchies between noise, sound and silence, the 1950s radio was of central importance to Cage's work because of its global or cosmic tentacles. If Cage was interested in a more central role for music in the 1950s, did this entail much more than a musical intervention into the communications' revolution, either by addressing new listening habits in the domestic sphere or exploring communications' potential to 'sonically map' expanded cosmological frontiers? To answer this question, it is helpful to start to address how Cage's thinking towards silence came together in the 1950s. Often mistakenly thought of as part of a sloppy 'anything goes' tendency to his work, silence, as John Hollander noted above, is the pattern to Cage's model. To do so, it is necessary to examine the pieces for radio that he composed in the decade.

It is possible to trace Cage's continued exploration of sound and domestic technologies throughout the 1950s: of the piano, the traditional instrument of the bourgeois 'drawing-room', the television and, most prominently, the radio. Cage persevered with an exploration of his notorious invention, the prepared piano – a grand piano manipulated to behave like a one-man percussion ensemble by the insertion of screws, bolts, pieces of wood and rubber between its strings. Work that had started in the *Imaginary Landscape* series also continued, using radio and phonograph as different sound sources that could be manipulated. He also explored the possibilities of amplification and spliced audio-tape to compose, among others, *Speech* (1955) for five radios and a newsreader; *Radio Music* (1956) lasting six minutes, for between one and eight performers, each at a radio; *Music Walk* (1958) for one or more pianists with radio and tape; and *Sounds of Venice* (1959), a television piece. His favourite and most famous piece, *4' 33"*, in which no sounds are to be produced intentionally, written for any instrument or combination of instruments, dates from 1952. As if to fulfil the maxim of Edgar Varese – 'the modern day composer refuses to die' – in Milan in 1958, during the composition of *Fontana Mix* for tape, Cage became a celebrity on Italian television by winning the American-style quiz show *Lascia o Raddoppia* ('Double or Nothing'). A curious event in the history of experimental music, and indeed in light entertainment, Cage answered all the first week's questions correctly after playing his *Amores* on prepared piano, a short piece that was a personal favourite of his compatriot, the folk singer Woody Guthrie. As Calvin Tomkins describes, after a set of questions the next week, Cage used the props department to perform the three-minute theatrical piece *Water Walk*, using objects associated with water, including a large rubber fish, a watering can and a pressure cooker.[12] Successfully naming, against the clock, all the species of white-spored mushrooms (mycology being his passionate interest and chosen specialist subject for the quiz), Cage won $6000 and returned home after turning down an offer to appear in Frederico Fellini's next film *La Dolce Vita*.

Frances Dyson traces the evolution of Cage's work with sounds in space from *Living Room Music*, written in 1940, to *Imaginary Landscape No. 4*, written in 1951.[13] In her essay, Dyson begins by suggesting that Cage's interest in sounds as objects and 'sounds in themselves' or, as Cage puts it, 'sounds, pure and simple'.[14] rather than as part of a harmonic system, is best seen as an exploration of 'abstracted spaces of technology'. This follows from Cage's attempts to explore sounds as objects by turning to percussion, as if to open up the 'spirit' of object through the sound it makes when struck. In *Living Room Music*, he instructs the performer to play the piece using, quite simply, objects found in a living room. Part of this new space of instrumentality, as Dyson calls it, would surely be the sound sources of the radio and television, those objects that literally act as mediums for other sounds. In *Living Room Music*, suggests Dyson:

> The music of the living room ... is reconfigured, transferred to the diaphanous field of the quasi-object, the object whose origins and ontology can be found in what Cage, referring to compositions produced 'when I was using electric or electronic technology', called 'Imaginary Landscapes'. From the prepared piano, to the living room, to the imaginary landscape, one can trace the course of both real and metaphorical space, phenomenal and symbolic meaning, as it continually abstracts and then redetermines what sounds, being themselves, might be. Sound is released first by an acoustic instrument, then by an electronic device; its being is connected first with silence, then with objects, and finally with technology; it is located at first in the orchestra, then in the living room, and finally, as the title of the compositions suggests, in the imagination.

This interaction between technology and the way sound is heard is one Cage suggests in his book *Silence*: 'Listening to this music one takes as a spring-board the first sound that comes along; the first something springs us into nothing and out of that nothing arises the next something, etc. like an alternating current.'[15]

The writings of Marshall McLuhan often feature prominently when discussing Cage's work with technology. In McLuhan's view, the older mechanical environment of a print-based culture was making way for a new environment of the new electronic media –

radio, television and telegraph. Regardless of the communicated content, our interaction with and through these technological surroundings inevitably changed our general perception in the latter half of the twentieth century. In both art and life, one could, according to McLuhan, detect a shift away from certain modes of thinking. As James Pritchett comments, quoting McLuhan: 'Print culture emphasised "*lineality* [sic], a one-thing-at-a-time awareness and mode of procedure" that included detached analysis, specialization, and fragmentation. The new electronic media, on the other hand, "deal in *auditory space*", with total involvement, unification and simultaneity.'[16]

Interest in McLuhan post-dates Cage's work on radio and is an extensive area for discussion. To focus on a few ideas, his writings provide an insight into Cage's shortwave radio pieces in the context of an emphasis on the increasingly globalised nature of post-war culture, a culture in which audio technology facilitated easier and swifter cross-global communications. It is important to emphasise that it was not the *message* being communicated that interested Cage and McLuhan, but the *medium* itself, because that shaped how the communication took place. On one level, Cage's radio 'compositions' attempted to demonstrate this, to foreground the medium over the message. Additionally, these compositions may have helped the listener to become aware of the prevalence of broadcast sound in everyday life, by mounting the domestic radio on a concert stage. But what is more fundamental to the 'compositions', as indeed to most of Cage's work, is their role in attempting to highlight the extension of everyday life and listening into this global, if not cosmic, realm. By enabling the almost unlimited dissemination of sound into space, broadcast technology allowed new connections to be made by the simple operation of the dial on a portable radio set.

Connecting what was once isolated through distance, the radio set was able to assemble a series of sounds from a huge variety of circulating sounds made portable through shortwave. Cage himself made grand claims for the compositional device he used to devise *Imaginary Landscape No. 4*. Numbers on the tuning dial are written out and chosen according to randomly generated charts created by the tossing of coins according to the I Ching procedure: 'It is thus possible to make a musical composition the continuity of which is free of individual taste and memory (psychology) and also of the literature and "tradition" of the art. The sounds enter the time-space centred within themselves, unimpeded by service to any abstraction, their 360 degrees of circumference free for an infinite play of penetration.'[17]

It was as if the radio could best manifest his philosophy, especially with its potential to be a medium for a 'music of the spheres'. Unlike the short range of FM, a sound broadcast from a single source of shortwave could be heard around the globe, across national boundaries. With the move away from linearity that McLuhan noted, an inability to signify inevitable historical progress, whether technological or moral, has its echoes in the open form of Cage's work. In this sense, his work can be placed productively in its decade. Shortwave radio production had been controlled during the Korean War. In an era of the military-industrial complex, America saw itself as the forerunner in technological progress, a progress displayed primarily through the 'space race' with the demonised Soviet Union. To incorporate shortwave broadcasts into his work, Cage was, in one sense, sharing the medium with the coded messages of Cold War espionage.

Cage's use of the radio in this era is, however, more complex. It is true that the introduction of unintended sounds into the performance of a piece enacts a faith in the complexities of experience against completeness and logical progression. It is also possible to relate the politics of his works to the dominant narratives of a Cold War history, as a curious attempt to disrupt its apparent continuities. But more is at stake than this. To argue that his work is politically counter-hegemonic would be to forget that it takes its place in an environment in which the aura of political and artistic intention wanes when reproduced and re-used. Testament to this is an example during World War II, in which the government used to broadcast Cage's work for prepared piano to the South Pacific 'with the hope of convincing the natives that America loves the Orient'.[18]

If we progress from the securities of artistic intention, we paradoxically move nearer to clarifying the extent of Cageian processes. In his description of *Imaginary Landscape No. 4* for twelve radios, Cage states: 'Value judgements are not in the nature of this work as regards either composition, performance, or listening. The idea of relation being absent, anything may happen. A "mistake" is beside the point, for once anything happens it authentically is.'[19] The premiere of *Imaginary Landscape No. 4* at Columbia University was considered a disaster by some.[20] Placed at the end of a rather long evening of music, most radio stations had gone off the air, resulting in a 'sparsely populated and hushed landscape'.[21] Cage's friend, the composer Morton Feldman, referred to such open-form work as being disaster-free. He states, 'What we learned was there are no catastrophes.'[22] What significance do these opinions have? Calvin Tomkins tells the story of a discussion Cage had with Gita Sarabhai, a young woman from a wealthy Indian family and one of his pupils at the New School. 'One day I asked what her teacher in India had thought was the purpose of music. She replied that he had said the function of music was "to sober and quiet the mind, thus rendering it susceptible to divine influences".'[23] Cage notes that he was 'tremendously struck by this'. Later, he confirmed this perspective, saying that music is 'a means of converting the mind, turning it around, so that it moves away from itself out of the rest of the world, or as Ramakrishna said, "as a means of rapid transportation"'.[24]

Listening to 'silence', or listening without structure and hierarchy, is then a means to opening up to a much larger context and understanding of a beyond. Indeterminacy worked in a similar way. Not a process to simply bypass conscious control in order to free the unconscious, as did Dada and Surrealism but, in an era in which popular Freudianism attempted to provide therapeutic answers to spiritual and everyday concerns, as a means to bypass the unconscious too. It is this emptiness of non-intention and non-hierarchy that comes nearer to achieving a role for listening that Cage believed could recreate a true 'music of the spheres' and that 'the Renaissance idea of self-expressive art was therefore heretical'.[25] The domestic radio encapsulated a vast range of unstructured sounds over vast spaces in the cosmos, a cosmos of complexity that dwarfed individual action. It was the ideal tool for such cosmic dimensions. In a certain sense, Cage's process of creation with radio mirrored the processes at work in the creation of the cosmos – an assembly of accidents governed by irrational laws. In another sense, his processes shared the arithmetic and systematic investigations of Pythagoras as he concluded that spheres must make sounds as they rotate in the heavens.[26] In his attempt to open up to spiritual concerns a technology that featured in everyday life of 1950s America, Cage offered to open an awareness of potential connections with further expedient complexities.

Notes

1. Robert Morgan (ed.), *Source Readings in Music History, Volume 7: The Twentieth Century*, (London, Norton, 1998).
2. Ibid., p. 196.
3. John Cage, *Silence* (London, Marion Boyars, 1978), p. 109.
4. Interesting parallels can be made here with the music of Stockhausen, particularly SPIRAL for a soloist with a short-wave radio receiver (1968).
5. Allan Kaprow, 'Right Living', in Jeff Kelley (ed.), *Essays on the Blurring of Art and Life* (London, University of California Press, 1993), pp. 223–4.
6. Calvin Tomkins, *The Bride and the Bachelors: The Heretical Courtship in Modern Art* (London, Weidenfeld and Nicolson, 1965), p. 133.
7. David Revill, *The Roaring Silence, John Cage: A Life* (London, Bloomsbury 1992), p. 185.
8. John Hollander, '*Silence*', in Richard Kostelanetz, *Writings About John Cage* (Ann Arbor, University of Michigan, 1993), p. 268.
9. '1950–1959 – Coming of Age', *Surfing the Aether*, www.the-bridge.net/~bchris/1950.htm.
10. 'Astronomy and Cosmology – The Nature of the Universe', *Pears Cyclopaedia* (1970–71) (London, Pelham Books, 1970).
11. '1950–1959 – Coming of Age'.
12. Tomkins, *The Bride and the Bachelors*, pp. 131–2.
13. Frances Dyson, 'The Ear that Would not Hear Sounds in Themselves: John Cage 1935–1965', in Douglas Kahn and Gregory Whitehead (eds), *Wireless Imagination: Sound, Radio and*

the Avant-Garde (London, Massachusetts Institute of Technology, 1992), pp. 373–407.
14. John Cage, *For The Birds* (London, Marion Boyars, 1981), p. 74.
15. Cage, *Silence*, p. 135.
16, Ibid., p. 151.
17. Ibid., p. 59.
18. Tomkins, *The Bride and the Bachelors* , p. 98.
19. Cage, *Silence*, p. 59.
20. Tomkins, *The Bride and the Bachelors*, p. 113.
21. James Pritchett, *The Music of John Cage* (Cambridge, Cambridge University Press, 1993), p. 90.
22. Tomkins, *The Bride and the Bachelors*, p. 109.
23. Ibid. p. 99.
24. Richard Kostelanetz, *Conversing with Cage* (London, Omnibus, 1989), p. 226.
25. Tomkins, *The Bride and the Bachelors*, p. 99.
26. Jamie James, *The Music of the Spheres: Music, Science and the Natural Order of the Universe* (London, Abacus, 1993).

CHAPTER SEVEN

'Only one way to fight a toxin': the poison and progress of radioactivity in *The Incredible Shrinking Man*

Kyle Smith

INTRODUCTION

The Incredible Shrinking Man (1957), directed by Jack Arnold and its screenplay written by Richard Matheson (based on Matheson's novel of the previous year), is one of more than a hundred science fiction films produced in America since the beginning of the 1950s.[1] It is the story of Scott Carey, who begins to shrink after a freak accident with an insect spray hideously altered by radiation. A one-in-a-million chance: just that amount of insecticide coupled with just that amount of radiation, received by his system in just that sequence and with just that timing. The radiation, dissipating quickly, becomes unnoticeable.[2] The narrative shows us the destruction of Carey's life by the accident, and his final philosophical reconciliation to his fate. Both book and film have received critical attention, most notably Barbara Creed's negative, feminist psychoanalytic reading of certain sections of the film[3], and Mark Jancovich's more positive reflections on representation of masculine anxiety in the fifties.[4] Certainly issues of gender are inescapable in the film, even more so than in the novel. As Jancovich puts it:

> [In the film] the process of transformation prior to Carey's descent into the world of the basement is of much less importance than his struggles once he finds himself in the cellar. The film is also far less concerned with a critique of Carey's need to hold on to specific notions of masculinity. Instead it presents

> the story as a regression from civilisation to primitivism, and ends up with a clearly religious return to the blissful union of man with the cosmos prior to the 'fall'.[5]

Gender issues, although still important in the film, retreat physically behind that perennial American male narrative of the hero's flight from domesticity, into what appears a pre-technological, prelapsarian world. This chapter will explore a factor that, although undoubtedly touched by issues of gender and technology, remains to be investigated more broadly: radiation.

During the 1950s, with America at the centre of a technological boom, the nation looked to the future with hope and anxiety. Not surprisingly, in the circumstances, the science fiction film flourished. Many of these films, in searching for newly discovered phenomena and topical hooks from the world of science, lighted on, not surprisingly, the discoveries of the atomic age and the power of radioactivity. *The Beast From 20,000 Fathoms* (1953), *The Creature From the Black Lagoon* (1954), *Them!* (1954), *Tarantula* (1955), *The Amazing Colossal Man* (1957) and *Attack of the 50 Foot Woman* (1958) all use radioactivity as a central catalyst to the action. Radioactivity has almost mystical properties and magical powers: it can make you bigger, it can make you smaller, it can turn you into a monster, or turn something else into a monster and turn you into a hero. Indeed, real radiation exposure had transformative effects – burns, hair loss, vomiting, organ and tissue degeneration, birth defects – but certainly not those that the cinema was interested in showing. Despite, or perhaps because of, the fear of radiation, fall out and apocalypse, these films tended to skirt, rather vicariously, the actualities. Radioactivity in these films is a *deus ex machina*, an excuse for otherwise impossible horrors, excitements and laughs. It is a product used to sell movies, a consumer product aimed at a particular market (usually the teenager) allowing a grotesqueness that the audience could identify with and narratives that made space for the audience to push themselves from the periphery of their communities to their centre. Radioactivity, like hormones and parents, seemed horrible and scary. Its true horridness remained garbled, for both adolescents and many of their elders.[6]

The Incredible Shrinking Man offers a view of radiation that fits easily into this picture: 'The film values innocence over knowledge, the undeveloped over the developed, and immaturity over maturity. While Carey is not a child at the end, he rejects the values of adult masculinity and maturity in favour of blissful union with creation.'[7] However, I want to use the film to draw parallels between its references to radiation and the general picture forming of radiation in the public domain. One of the reasons we can do this is because the film allows its exposed hero to survive, while most irradiated parties in these films, for safety's sake, tend to die. This allows us a unique journey through some of America's perceptions of atomic energy and its particularly virulent waste product.

ATOMIC TESTS

From the opening credits of the film, a sense of the anxiety of the atomic age comes to the forefront. Initially, we see a white figure on the left-hand side of the screen shrinking against a black background, while in the centre, a tiny white, post-nuclear cloud increases in size. If it is not such an apocalyptic cloud that floats over Carey's boat in the opening scenes of the film, it still proves to be radioactive. With these credits and opening scenes, it would be easy to see radiation as being at the centre of the movie; in a sense it is, as the medical experts will discover that this cloud has a central role to play in Scott Carey's shrinking. However, past the 'acid sting'[8] of what appears to the untrained eye to be some sort of silver, party glitter (more like fairy dust than fallout), the cloud remains an extremely indistinct phenomenon. It is one that Carey's fellow passenger (the brother in the book, and the wife in the film) is able to avoid by staying off deck for a matter of seconds. Carey even manages to forget completely about the incident until prompted by the doctors. The question of radiation, like the cloud itself, drifts out of sight without really ever having been confronted. At no point has anyone seemed the least interested in what a radioactive cloud is doing floating off the American coast. I am merely surmising that is where they are, but it is a small boat, belonging to Carey's brother, unlikely to be moored far from home.

Although the other aspect of the deadly cocktail, the insecticide, is pinpointed quite exactly ('Los Angeles, a Saturday afternoon'[9]), neither the film nor the book specify exactly the site of the radioactive encounter.

So where did this cloud come from? We cannot really say, but we can chart some of the sites where radioactivity was being produced in abundance. By the time of Eisenhower's election as president, America had already stockpiled 1000 nuclear warheads, weapons whose capacity was being constantly developed under a rigorous testing campaign. Although sixty-six nuclear blasts took place on Bikini Atoll and Eniwetok from 1948 to 1958, much of the testing in the early 1950s moved to the American mainland for the first time, mainly for security reasons. The move to the Nevada Desert saw a new phase in nuclear testing:

> The new program called for the purposeful, systematic exposure of American and Canadian servicemen and personnel to the direct effects of atomic bombs. The army's newly formed Human Resources and Research Office needed to gather detailed data on motivation, morale psychology, and training methods most useful for troops engaging in nuclear war. From 1951 and on through the decade between 250 000 and 500 000 servicemen were exposed to the effects of atomic bombs in the more than one hundred tests conducted. Countless civilians located in the path of the fallout were also exposed, but apparently the collecting of data on them was of less interest to the military.[10]

Eisenhower, when confronted with the dangers to citizens living near test sites, is alleged to have said, 'We can afford to sacrifice a few thousand people out there in the interests of national security.'[11]

In our present age of constant litigation against State and Corporation, Carey's lack of interest in where the cloud comes from seems quaint and naive. But it reflects, aside from any issues of censorship, a representation of radiation as a force, not so much of military and government planning, but of nature. In both the book and the film, the cloud takes on a sourcelessness, a randomness that one might associate with a natural disaster. Here, radioactivity is a force beyond our control. For those with an investment in a permanent war economy, an economy with the atomic bomb at its centre, it was an appearance they were happy to see maintained.

RADIOACTIVITY AND MEDICINE

The medical profession, as reflected in the case of Scott Carey, seems as uninterested as the military in the effect of radioactivity on civilians. Although the medical experts are presented fairly positively, they are unable to help Carey, and soon they drift out the picture. However, they are still connected closely to the question of radiation, but in a more progressive sense. These medical figures offer a more controlled picture of the progress of radioactivity and, although in the novel Carey grows tired of his hospitalisation,[12] in the film it becomes an opportunity for the camera to dwell on a number of scientific tests: radioactive iodine, barium meals, Geiger counters and X-rays. Here, radioactivity exists as a force utilised and controlled to discover the source of his illness: these are not toxins for they discover toxins. Our medics fight fire with fire, using the tracing properties of radioactivity to find the radiation at the source of Carey's illness.[13]

The medical experts disappear quickly after they have discovered the 'new toxin'[14] in Carey's system, what is termed in the film his 'anti-cancer'. The medical experts' anti-toxin to this anti-cancer, with its short period of success, emphasises the limitation of their powers in the face of something beyond them. Rather than one form of technology outstripping another, science, in general, seems humbled. The very professionalism of the medical men trying to help Carey proves the superior power of this freak accident, distancing it from the forces of technology, until it can only be termed an act of 'nature'. While Carey begins to shrink once more, the medical fraternity vanish altogether, apparently uninterested in this new form of radioactivity and those they cannot help to get better. They are not even inquisitive enough to do an autopsy on the family cat, which Carey's wife imagines, wrongly, has eaten her husband. Such a picture of doctors interested only in helping the sick get well is at odds with the complete picture concerning radioactivity and medicine at the time. Although it might appear that the military and the president were uninterested in the effects of radioactivity on the civilian, the medical world did take an interest. After all, the assembly-line construction of nuclear weapons demands workers who, inevitably, will come into contact with these dangerous substances.[15] Recent American government reports have shown that in the 1950s doctors in radioactive research used civilians:

> From 1945 through 1947, Manhattan Project researchers injected eighteen human subjects with plutonium, five human subjects with polonium, and six human subjects with uranium to obtain metabolic data related to the safety of those working on the production of nuclear weapons. All of these subjects were patients hospitalised at facilities affiliated with the Universities of Rochester, California, and Chicago or at Oak Ridge. Another set of experiments took place between 1953 and 1957 at Massachusetts General Hospital, in which human subjects were injected with uranium. In no case was there any expectation that these patient-subjects would benefit medically from the injections.[16]

Carey, victim of an indeterminate radioactive cloud, is shown his disease through medicine's own radioactive tests (tests that, in reality, were utilising radioactivity's effect not just to identify other diseases in the body but to further the knowledge of the nuclear industry). Arnold (the film's director) and Matheson (screenplay writer and author of the original book) show us a benign medical fraternity that is finally powerless in the face of a power that appears beyond man, not created by man. Science, as they show it, does not appear to meddle with what it does not understand entirely.

THE ATOMIC AND THE DOMESTIC

These experiments were secret, and suppression of information was at the centre of the continuing atomic programme. Those most fearful of the bomb falling into the wrong hands, and those interested in a permanent war economy, tried to repress information that might turn the public against the bomb. Much of the footage from Hiroshima and Nagasaki remained censored through the 1950s: 'The US military confiscated some 45 000 feet of documentary footage shot by Japanese producer Akira Iwasaki during the immediate aftermath of the Hiroshima bombing. This footage also remained classified for decades. In 1946, when Japanese doctors attempted to release their own detailed documentation on radiation-related diseases, this information was also censored by the US occupation forces.'[17]

Had, as Nelson says, 'the dangers of radiation, documented in Japan from 1946 onward, not been suppressed and censored by the United States, it is doubtful whether the nuclear juggernaut could have advanced as it did. Keeping the secret of radiation's deadliness was of crucial importance in the immediate post-war years.'[18]

Beyond the military and the government situation, few routes seemed to offer much clarity. The media swung between massively optimistic views of the effect of radiation (*Time* magazine wrote in 1961 that ninety per cent of the population could survive nuclear attack in fallout shelters) and widely paranoid fears of apocalypse (following the explosion of Russia's first nuclear bomb, with the launch of Sputnik). In such wildly differing reactions growing out of various agendas, more informative views could easily be lost. For instance, in September 1952, *Life* magazine circulated a photo essay on disfigured survivors of Hiroshima and Nagasaki; and in May 1955, a disturbing Atomic Energy Commission report came out, admitting an underestimation in the level of effects caused by fallout. The secrecy, ambiguity and uncertainty of the government, the military, the media and the scientific establishment affected the public's ability to gain much of a perspective on the nuclear deterrent.[19]

But it was not just a matter of hiding the threat of radiation. It was necessary to find methods of articulating radiation in a positive way, of connecting it to every day life. In a sense, Scott Carey's condition brings radiation into everyday life; radiation becomes a catalyst for dealing with the nature of masculinity in sexual and other social situations. Carey reflects the attempt to connect radiation to our everyday life, but also he parallels, in his very exposure to radiation, the difficulty of representing a phenomena that is unknown to us or difficult to perceive.

Though not dealt with in the intense fashion of the novel, masculinity is still apparent in the film in a sort of visual shorthand. The film pares down Carey's social world and the physical space he moves through: the introductory scenes are singular in the openness and freedom of their setting, while the rest of the film is spent mostly in the Careys' lounge or cellar. We are presented with Carey at particularly shocking stages of diminution, revolving around the relationship of man and wife and how this might define him as a male. Thus, one of the first moments when the change in Carey comes home is when his wedding ring slips off his finger; the first time we see Carey noticeably smaller, the size of a child, he is being told he has lost his job. What is maintained, emphasised and exaggerated throughout this is the fact that we are in a domestic scene. This visual stripping away of what defines Carey as a man takes place within the oppressiveness and claustrophobia of an inescapable home environment associated, in its American cultural context, with the female. In the film, the shrinking is played out in terms of the environment Carey moves through, something that, although present in the novel, is given greater emphasis in the visual form. In one scene we see Carey sitting, almost lost, on the sofa, almost trapped behind the weight of a giant book. Throughout the film, the camera continues a narrative of physical comparison, even to represent Carey's social world. Carey is the perfect character to bring out this because he is constantly defining himself by comparison, in the most hierarchical of fashions. Carey's initial horrors are his clothes being too big for him and his wife not having to stretch to kiss him. As we watch Carey shrink to the size of a child, the comparisons are there for us to make: Carey is compared to chairs and telephones and coffee cups and radios: it is the most potent way of charting his reduction. While the pressures of his position distance him increasingly from human contact, these are the only things he has any relationship with. They remind him constantly of his infantilisation; as special effects they give us not only the sense of Carey growing smaller but the dual effect, in the reality of these objects being oversized, of the world that these objects project getting bigger, more important and out of his control.

We need a context to see, to understand, to explain what is happening to Carey, what the radiation has done to him. Similarly, it is in the best interests of the authorities not only to withhold information, but also to articulate the nature of the power of the atomic bomb. In a sense, their secrecy can be justified as a necessity to keep the bomb in their safe and capable hands, but also we must see the nation's power ('our' power) in ways the citizens understand and in ways that will make them secure in the certainty of its control. Especially with the moving of nuclear tests to the mainland, there had to be some attempt to explain both the power and safety to the public. Selected journalists were allowed to witness these new mainland tests through 1951 into 1952. Also in 1952, the Atomic Energy Commission allowed the first public television coverage of a bomb test.[20] Such public shows continued through the 1950, including this test outlined by Dale Carter:

> In 1955, Operation Cue was set up by the government as a public relations exercise designed to give the man in the street a sense of the bomb's power. In Operation Cue, some 200 companies decorated the blast area with their various consumer products in order to test their durability and reliability under demanding conditions while television commentators and press men crouched in a trench two miles from Ground Zero waiting to publicise the results.[21]

Here, an attempt is made to make the bomb more 'accessible'. We can see it in terms of everyday items, see how its power destroys these things. The removal of the humans who buy and use these consumer products makes the comparisons more interestingly abstract, more palatable. Yet one cannot help thinking of this representing the domestic scene itself. As with Carey, showing the external world expanding out of control, the test also brings home its opposite. The surreal site of consumer durables littering test sites connects us to the idea of a real atomic explosion and the destruction of the contents of our own homes. It mirrors an apocalyptic aftermath. These attempts to articulate the force of the bomb – emphasising its power and the military's control, de-emphasising the threat to human life and the environment – convey uncertainty as well as certainty. It tells us nothing about the bomb that we want to know; it tells us things that deflect us from asking the things we need to know. We see nothing but the event; we learn nothing about the phenomena, except its power, that it is 'our' power. In a sense, this is also what has happened with Scott Carey: here, also, the event of shrinking, and its representation, replaces the phenomenon that caused it.

THE ATOMIC, NATURE AND GOD

The second half of the film, after the point at which Carey's wife imagines that he has been killed by the family cat, is about Carey regaining some sort of control. In the first half of the movie, as Carey shrinks, his world shrinks. Once in the cellar, though, he loses all relationship with humanity and the cellar world expands, as he no longer comes into contact with a social world based on expectations, competition and comparisons. Carey has grown so small that everything is strange to him: his wife's pins, needles and thread become swords, grappling hooks and rope. As weapons with which to fight the spider, his major foe and benchmark in this part of the film, these items lose their domestic connotations. Where the consumer objects upstairs had become, for Carey, articles by which he unhappily compared and defined himself, the cellar objects have to be adapted, rather than consumed: Carey thus defines them, creates them. Carey's fight with the spider sees him face up to his fears, rather than hiding behind predefined roles that demand he have no fears. In the struggle in the cellar and the defeat of the spider, Carey finally defeats his 'toxic introspections'.[22] What the book terms his 'jungle life'[23], and what the film reflects in thirty minutes of near silent activity (as he searches for food and plans the destruction of the spider) in the cellar, seems to release him from social anxieties – familiar contemporary anxieties, not so much created by his shrinking as exacerbated to an unbearable level by it.

This new relationship to hierarchies that shrinking finally brings for Carey, represented to us through the special effects, is somewhat compromised in the end. The closing scene puts Carey back out in the open again, but without his wife. She has left the scene some time ago, presuming him dead. Carey's final fluidity of meaning and anti-hierarchical stance is very radical, very beat generation in the beatific sense, yet it is achieved by merely removing the most troublesome of elements from the equation (gender and capitalism) and replacing them with God, nature and universal meaning. And it is not merely that, finally, we have just another 'melodrama of beset manhood'; [24] that Carey cannot be reconciled to the gendered world because he cannot break its association with the bourgeois one. There is still the problem of radioactivity as well.

The close of the film, even more than the opening and the sections of medical investigation, turns the radioactivity affecting Carey into a force of nature that can be reacted to only passively. At the tumultuous finale, ringing with biblical music, our hero grown so small that his rags appear the robes of a prophet, Carey has cut all connections with every social force standing between him and God. In the book, the final force seems less specifically religious, although the final speech of the film is culled from much of the dialogue, tending to substitute God for nature:

> He stood again. Why had he never thought of it; of the microscopic and the submicroscopic worlds? That they existed he had always known. Yet never had he made the obvious connection. He'd always thought in terms of man's own world and man's own limited dimensions. He had presumed upon nature. For the inch was man's concept, not nature's. To a man, zero inches mean nothing. Zero meant nothing. But to nature there was no zero. Existence went on in endless cycles. It seemed so simple now. He would never disappear, because there was no point of non-existence in the universe. It frightened him at first. The idea of going on endlessly through one level of dimension after another was alien.[25]

It is a picture that is both more social ('He might not have to be alone.'[26]) and less static ('Scott Carey ran into a new world, searching.'[27]).

The novel emphasises a universe made up of endless un-hierarchical levels of existence as opposed to the film's circle of 'infinitesimal and infinite', but both show Carey humbled, realising he has 'presumed on nature'.[28] That his experience should humble him personally is perhaps not surprising. That it is nature he sees as the source of his transformation is misleading but certainly understandable within the parameters of the story. What is finally amazing is that he chooses to see what has happened to him as having a positive long-term result for humankind: that the radiation bursts might have been repeated all over the world and have created a new race: that he is the 'man of the future'.

Now, Carey is indeed a man of the future, in the sense that today, well nigh all of us have been exposed to our own cocktails of strontium-90 and pesticides.[29] Some interested parties might say it is of little harm, but no one would say we were the better for it. For Carey, exposure becomes the best thing that could have happened to him, a misfortune of biblical proportions that leads him on the true path. Radiation can, of course, be natural, but the radiation that was full of symbolism in the 1950s for its magical powers, its awesome strength, its terrible capabilities, is man-made, American-made. While *The Incredible Shrinking Man* can no longer reconcile itself to career, or consumer culture, or marriage, it attempts reconciliation with nature. However, it is a rather tenuous, ambiguous link with nature, dependent as it is with a phenomenon linked to technology. What we have, not for the first time in American culture, is technology mistaken for nature.

In fact, Carey's final progression might be seen in terms of another move beyond the American sublime, awe in the face of nature's vastness and power. Leo Marx saw awesome images of technology replacing images of the pastoral at the turn of the century declaring America's sense of national power.[30] Here we have images, at source technological, being mistaken for the natural: a technological sublime of a different order, perhaps the first intimations of a post-modern notion of the sublime in the atomic age, what Rob Wilson terms 'techno-euphoria'.[31]

Carey is finally reduced to his essence by radioactivity. What

Carey has is not cancer but an 'anti cancer', a reduction in nitrogen, creatinine, phosphorus and calcium.[32] Whereas in cancer one has a proliferation of cancer cells (that is, cells that grow without dying, eventually destroying all others), we have an impossibly proportional reduction of bone and muscle growth. In fact, what the film seems to suggest is that Carey shrinks to a single-cell organism. What infects Carey does not 'take him over'. Rather, it reduces him to his essence, to a single unit both unique and integrated within 'God's rich tapestry'. This atomisation might be compared to the molecularisation of information and duties associated with the Fordist order that Carey appears to be fleeing. This order is epitomised by security surrounding atomic research from the Manhattan Project onwards, exemplified by a quote from General Leslie R. Groves, the military head of the Manhattan Project: 'Compartmentalization of knowledge, to me, was the very heart of security. My rule was simple and not capable of misinterpretation – each man should know everything he needed to do his job and nothing else.'[33]

Carey, seeing two faces in the one monolith, both flees this order and embraces it, but in his nature he contradicts the very foundations on which it is based. Despite his reduction to the most simplistic and utilitarian unit in God's universe, his reduction is caused by radioactivity. And why is this important? Because radioactivity, from our introduction to the cloud in the credits, remains connected to the humanly created waste product associated with the splitting of the atom, the splitting of the smallest of perceived units. Carey is made singular by exposure to the process that refutes singularity. The attempt to become or create the smallest component of control in the name of personal or national security becomes linked inextricably to the destruction of the concept of such a unit. The atomic age is not the age of the atom but the age of its instability, the impossibility of its singularity, the potential for multiplicity.[34]

CONCLUSION

It was only after World War II that radiation as a cultural construct came into the public domain. Although radiation is emitted by a number of natural sources, and has been known about and studied in various forms since the nineteenth century, its presence is most widely regarded in terms of the emission of particles and rays in nuclear decay. Generally, in the 1950s, and to a large extent today, it is associated, almost exclusively, with atomic energy, the splitting of the atom, the atomic bomb. With the incredibly successful secrecy of the Manhattan Project, the atom bomb and what its power entailed came into the public domain with a unique suddenness. Articulating what the bomb was and did proved a difficult and ambiguous task.[35] Truman described the bomb dropped on Hiroshima as 'the greatest thing in history'.[36] John Hersey, writing in his 1946 essay on devastated Hiroshima, captures some of this ambiguity when he writes that the citizens of the city were 'the objects of the first great experiment in the use of atomic power, which ... no country except the United States, with its industrial know-how, its willingness to throw two billion dollars into an important wartime gamble, could possibly have developed'.[37] Americans found themselves both in awe of the bomb's power and fearful of its consequences, proud of its invention in America and hopeful that its nuclear power would have more positive effects – but also scared it might fall into the wrong hands.

The Incredible Shrinking Man heads towards atomisation as a site of containment, safety, a way of looking at an ever more complicated world, in terms of sexuality, prosperity and foreign policy, with some sort of personal and national sense of security. Yet at this very point, Carey is victim of the atom's ability to be no longer singular, to be split and to be fused, the radioactive by-product of which, in a cultural sense, is the starting point of the shrinking narrative. The film and the book, both successful, reveal the consensus view that government, military and science wished to project of atomic energy and its waste products as dangerous but useful, an awesome, frightening force that could be controlled. They also reveal the contradictions and dualities of that power by placing radiation back in the 'hands' of the force from which, scientists said, it was being harnessed. This, of course, is nature, the place where that which frightens and excites the American white male appears repeatedly.[38] Carey's predicament reflects an American policy of secrecy, manipulation and control of information that sought to make atomic power appear as a force safe in good Christian hands, but also one that should, for security's sake, 'passeth all understanding', In putting radiation back in the hands of God, *The Incredible Shrinking Man* reflects both the attempts to control information and the failure to do so seamlessly.[39] Carey's story offers a route in which to follow the perception of radioactivity in the public domain: the contradictions of its presentation, the anxieties and delusions it propagates, all in the name of a State organised increasingly along the lines of a permanent war economy. There might be, as Matheson's novel suggests, 'only one way to fight a toxin, and that was with an antitoxin'[40], but selling a toxin demands a number of integrated strategies which always threaten to reveal their contradictions.

Notes

1. Dale Carter, *The Final Frontier: The Rise and Fall of the American Rocket State* (London, Verso, 1988), p. 94.
2. Richard Matheson, *The Incredible Shrinking Man* (Sphere, 1988), p. 119.
3. Barbara Creed, *The Monstrous Feminine: Film, Feminism, Psychoanalysis* (London, Routledge, 1993).
4. Mark Jancovich, *Rational Fears: American Horror in the 1950s* (Manchester, Manchester University Press, 1996).
5. Ibid., pp. 191–2.
6. 'The 1950s were difficult and changing times for the movie companies. The increasing surburbanisation of the prospering population and the rise of the television saw the decline of the mass audience for the cinema. It became necessary to target audiences in the depleting market. This often benefited smaller independent producers, the low budget wings of the big movie producers and the teenage audiences who wanted to differentiate themselves from their elders: these films also become bound up with youth cultures through their preoccupation with alienated outsiders. Their isolated figures

who were abused by the guardians of normality, for no other reason than their freakish difference, was a point of identification for a generation of youth who were trying to articulate their dissatisfactions with the values of middle-class America. Indeed, these films covertly discussed these issues of difference in terms of developmental metaphors, which explored the standards of maturity that regulated the social codes of 1950s behaviour.' Jancovich, *Rational Fears*, p. 169.

7. Jancovich, *Rational Fears*, p. 194.
8. Matheson, *The Incredible Shrinking Man*, p. 119.
9. Ibid.
10. Joyce Nelson, 'TV, the Bomb, and the Body: Other Cold War Secrets', in Marjorie Garber and Rebecca L. Walkowitz (eds), *Secret Agents: The Rosenberg Case, McCarthyism and Fifties America* (London, Routledge, 1995), pp. 32–45. Nelson's chapter is a central source to this essay. It captures the extent to which the corporate business community was interested in creating a permanent war economy, interlocking it into the fears and machinations of politicians and the actual threat that Russia posed: all major factors in the creation of the Cold War.
11. Carole Galbraith, *American Ground Zero: The Secret Nuclear War* (Cambridge, USA, Massachusetts Institute of Technology Press, 1993), p. xxviii.
12. 'I'm tired of being tested,' he went on, not wanting to sink into comfortless isolation of silence again. 'I'm tired of basal-metabolism tests and protein-bound tests; tired of drinking radioactive iodine and barium-powdered water; tired of X-rays and blood cultures and Geiger counters on my throat and having my temperature taken a million times a day. You haven't been through it; you don't know. It's like an inquisition. And what the hell's the point? They haven't found a thing. Not a thing! And they never will. And I can't see owing them thousands of dollars for nothing!' Matheson, *The Incredible Shrinking Man*, p. 119.
13. 'You have a negative nitrogen balance, Mr Carey. Your body is throwing off more nitrogen than it is retaining. Since nitrogen is one of the major building blocks of the body, consequently we have shrinkage... An imbalance of creatinine was causing further involution. Phosphorus and calcium were being thrown off, too, in the precise proportion in which those elements were found in his bones... A poison that, without destroying the pituitary gland, destroyed, little by little, its ability to maintain

growth. A poison that day by day forced his system to convert nitrogen into waste matter; a poison that affected creatinine and phosphorus and calcium and left them as waste to be thrown off.' Matheson, *The Incredible Shrinking Man*, pp. 117–19.

14. Matheson, *The Incredible Shrinking Man*, p. 118.
15. Nelson, 'TV, the Bomb, and the Body: Other Cold War Secrets', pp. 34–5.
16. 'The Advisory Committee is persuaded that these experiments were motivated by a concern for national security and worker safety and that, particularly in the case of the plutonium injections, they produced results that continue to benefit workers in the nuclear industry today. However, with the possible exception of the polonium experiments, we believe that these experiments were unethical. In the conduct of these experiments, two basic moral principles were violated – that one ought not to use people as a mere means to the ends of others and that one ought not to deceive others – in the absence of any morally acceptable justification for such conduct. National security considerations may have required keeping secret the names of classified substances, but they would not have required using people as subjects in experiments without their knowledge or giving people the false impression that they or their family members had been given treatment when instead they had been given a substance that was not intended to be of benefit.' 'Uranium was also injected into eleven patients with terminal conditions at Massachusetts General Hospital in an experiment conducted jointly by the hospital and Oak Ridge National Laboratory [ORNL] from 1953 to 1957. ORNL's purpose was to obtain data for setting nuclear worker safety standards. A second purpose was to identify a radioisotope that would localise in brain tumors and destroy them when activated by a neutron beam. Although all but one of the patient-subjects had brain cancer, the limited purpose of the experiment – to establish whether uranium would localize sufficiently – meant that there was no expectation that patient-subjects might benefit medically from the uranium injections.' These quotes, and that in the text, are taken from the conclusion of the Advisory Committee on Human Radiation Experiments (ACHRE) Final Report. On 15 January 1994, President Clinton appointed the ACHRE to investigate reports of possibly unethical experiments funded by the government in the 1940s and

1950s. It is published on the Web site of the Office of Human Radiation Experiments, which was established in March 1994 as part of the American Department of Energy's attempts to record the agency's Cold War record on radiation research: http://tis-nt.eh.doe.gov/ohre/roadmap/achre/chap5_5.html.

17. Nelson, 'TV, the Bomb, and the Body: Other Cold War Secrets', p. 36.
18. Ibid., p. 9.
19. Carter, *The Final Frontier*, pp. 103–8.
20. Nelson, 'TV, the Bomb, and the Body: Other Cold War Secrets', p. 40.
21. Carter, *The Final Frontier*, p. 103.
22. Matheson, *The Incredible Shrinking Man*, p. 108.
23. Matheson, *The Incredible Shrinking Man*, p. 75.
24. Nina Baym, *Feminism and American Literary History* (New Brunswick, Rutger University Press, 1992), pp. 4–18.
25. Matheson, *The Incredible Shrinking Man*, p. 216.
26. Ibid.
27. Ibid.
28. Ibid.
29. As Jim Falk points out, 'Everybody on earth now has strontium-90 in their body tissues.' This is quoted from Falk's keynote paper to The World Uranium Hearing in Salzburg in 1992, a conference set up to give scientific, historical and first-hand accounts of environmental and personal abuse suffered out of the misuses of nuclear power. The paper can be found in a collection of papers from the conference, entitled *Poison Fire, Sacred Earth*, but I lifted this particular section from the Internet: http://www.suburbia.com.au/~suzieq/chapters/uranium/JimFalk.html.
30. Leo Marx, *The Machine in the Garden: Technology and the Pastoral Ideal in America* (London, Oxford University Press, 1964).
31. Rob Wilson, 'Techno-Euphoria and the Discourse of the American Sublime', in Edward E. Pease (ed.), *National Identities and Post-Americanist Narratives* (London, Duke University Press, 1994), pp. 205–29.
32. Matheson, *The Incredible Shrinking Man*, p. 117.
33. Quoted in Nelson, 'TV, the Bomb, and the Body: Other Cold War Secrets', p. 34.
34. In a sense, the book is superior to the film in that it shows this contradiction more clearly. The anti-hierarchical endings of the book and the film show how the splitting of the atom could

open up considerations of whole new strata of the universe, rather than reintroduce us to pantheism.

35. This was true even though the dangers that the bomb contained became clear almost immediately. As Jim Falk writes: 'By 1939, Otto Hahn had split uranium atoms by bombarding them with other bits of radiation, neutrons. And Fermi and Szilard had begun to build an atomic pile to utilize the chain reaction. And a year later, Otto Frisch and Rudolf Pierls described in a three-page paper how uranium-235 could be assembled into a critical mass producing an atomic explosion. And they noted: "In addition to the destructive effects of the explosion itself, the whole material of the bomb would be transformed into a highly radioactive state. The energy radiated by these active substances will amount to about twenty percent of the energy liberated in the explosion, and the radiation would be fatal to living beings even a long time after the explosion." So, as early as that we had very much the picture of the atomic bomb. And it didn't stay just on paper: the most dramatic demonstration was on the 6th of August, 1945, when a uranium bomb was dropped on Hiroshima on 400,000 people. 20,000 died in the explosion and heat of the blast. Another bomb made from plutonium was dropped on Nagasaki. By the end of the year, 120,000 people were dead at Hiroshima, a further 70,000 at Nagasaki had died from the effects of the bomb.' http://www.suburbia.com.au/~suzieq/chapters/uranium/JimFalk.html.
36. Quoted in H. Montgomery Hyde, *The Atom Bomb Spies* (London, Hamish Hamilton, 1980), p. 222. In a filmic sense, one has only to see Gary Cooper describing the nature of the 'thing' in the truly dire *Cloak and Dagger* (dir. Fritz Lang, 1947): 'Look, in a few years, maybe, we will be able to break up the atomic structure of this apple,' says Cooper, playing a nuclear physicist, holding up the piece of fruit. 'When we do that, it will become a bomb.'
37. John Hersey, *Hiroshima* (London, Penguin, 1986), p. 71.
38. Matheson, *The Incredible Shrinking Man*, p. 119.
39. Wilson, 'Techno-Euphoria and the Discourse of the American Sublime', p. 208.
40. In one sense, we might think this places Carey squarely with the Beats, in the beatific sense: 'Recent history is the record of a vast conspiracy to impose one level of mechanical consciousness on mankind and exterminate all manifestations of

that unique part of human sentience, identical in all men, which the individual shares with his creator,' so said Ginsberg in 1959 [Allen Ginsberg, 'Poetry, Violence and the Trembling Lambs', in Thomas Parkinson (ed.), *A Casebook on the Beat* (New York, Thomas T. Crowell Company, 1965), p. 24.]. Perhaps *The Incredible Shrinking Man* reflects a reaction to that state of affairs. Yet while appearing to flee the image of Fordist representations like William Whyte's Organisation Man, Carey can also resemble this figure and his 'social ethic', which is 'a belief in the group as the source of creativity; a belief in "belongingness" as the ultimate need of the individual; and a belief in the application of science to achieve belongingness'. Whether Carey finally has stopped being an Organisation Man is a moot point: we could say that he has joined a bigger Organisation. William H. Whyte, Jr, *The Organization Man*, (London, Jonathan Cape Ltd, 1957), p. 7.

CHAPTER EIGHT

Muscular manhood and salacious sleaze: the singular world of the 1950s macho pulps

Bill Osgerby

'We must face the dynasty of the dames at once, deprive them of our pocketbooks when they waste the substance in them, and take back our dreams which, without the perfidious materialism of mom, were shaping up a new and braver world. We must drive roads to Rio and to Moscow and stop spending all our strength in the manufacture of girdles: it is time that mom's sag became known to the desperate public; we must plunge into our psyches and find out there, each for each, scientifically, about immortality and miracles. To do such deeds, we will first have to make the conquest of momism, which grew up from male default.'[1]

THE MACHO PULPS AND THE DYNASTY OF THE DAMES

One of the more curious publishing phenomena of post-war America was the rise of the 'men's true adventure magazine'. From the 1940s through to the mid-1960s, the pages of titles such as *True Adventures*, *Man's Life*, *Stag* and *Action for Men* were home to a bizarre, often grotesque, world of swaggering machismo, prurient voyeurism and sexual violence. A cheap and garish publishing genre, these 'macho pulps' (as they could be loosely termed[2]) offered a potent cocktail of melodrama, brutality and lurid sleaze. Their stock in trade was gritty action and tawdry sex. Purportedly 'true' tales of wartime heroics and the testing of manhood ('There Were Only 12 of Us – Against 5000 Nazi Beasts!', 'My 57 Bloody Days at Dien Bien Phu') appeared alongside 'glamour model' photo-spreads, steamy exposés of lasciviousness and debauchery ('Sex Cult Sin Parties', 'Exposed: The Truth About Love-Hungry Divorcees') and a range of fiction and feature articles dealing with crime-fighting, hunting, exploration, sport and other suitably 'manly' pursuits. The macho pulps were, above all, champions of a no-nonsense brand of ruggedly heterosexual masculinity, proffering – as the publishers of *Man's Illustrated* put it – 'true adventures for bold men'.

Yet behind the macho pulps' celebration of tough-guy bravado and boisterous lechery there lurked nagging doubts and anxieties. The blustering claims to an exaggerated form of robust and virile manhood disguised a profound sense of unease and insecurity, which occasionally surfaced more explicitly in the magazines' enquiring features and 'self-test' articles dealing with issues of character and sexuality ('How Tough Do You Think You Really Are?', 'Can You Meet a Woman's Most Intimate Needs?', 'Are You a Potential Homosexual?'). In these terms, the macho pulps testified to wider fears and uncertainties that characterised American society during the Cold War era.

Contrary to popular perceptions of the 1950s as a time of relative tranquillity and consensus in the USA, historians have increasingly shown the period to be 'an era of conflict and contradiction, an era in which a complex set of ideologies contended for public allegiance'.[3] Authors such as Lary May[4] and Joanne Meyerowitz[5] have highlighted the way in which processes of flux and fragmentation were endemic to American public and private life throughout the period, as the global tensions of the Cold War, the rise of domestic consumption, changes in gender roles and the gradual emergence of civil rights activism and other movements of popular protest contributed to a climate of social stress and apprehension. These anxieties became especially manifest in the realm of sexual politics. As Jeffrey Weeks has shown perceptively, debates about sexuality invariably possess an important symbolic dimension.[6] Touching on crucial social boundaries and provoking intimate questions about personal identity, issues of gender and sexuality often come to condense a wider set of concerns about the nature and pace of social change.

This was clearly the case in post-war America. In a period of dramatic national and international change, anxiety and unease cohered around a perceived breakdown in traditional gender identities. Changes in women's social and economic roles aroused particular disquiet. During wartime, entry into the labour force or living alone as a wife or mother had been an empowering experience for many women. In peacetime, however, such independence was seen as a threat to the stability of the traditional sexual order, and government and industry united in a campaign to return women to the home and the secure confines of the nuclear family.[7] The impact of post-war social life on norms of masculinity also aroused alarm and suspicion. Trends towards suburbanisation, growing domestic comfort and the rise of faceless bureaucracies appeared to be sapping the American male's traditional vigour. Even worse, it seemed to many influential commentators that men were being robbed of their masculine dynamism by doting mothers and hectoring wives. In these terms, then, a combination of white-collar bureaucrats and domineering women threatened to emasculate American manhood. In response, the restoration and revitalisation of traditional gender roles came to be seen as a vital task if America was to sustain its position as a pre-eminent economic power and bastion of the 'free world'. The macho pulps represented one (particularly sordid and misogynistic) facet of this post-war effort to 'reclaim' American masculinity.

GREY-FLANNEL BREADWINNERS AND THE DECLINE OF THE AMERICAN MALE

The post-war macho pulp magazines can be located in the longer history of American 'pulp' publishing. According to aficionados, the heyday of the pulp was the 1920s and 1930s, a time when news-stands were thronged with literally hundreds of cheap, yet visually striking, magazines bearing titles such as *Argosy*, *Astounding Stories*, *Ace Detective* and *Spicy Mystery Stories*. By the 1950s, the age of the pulp magazine was, according to the genre's 'official' historians, over, the market falling prey to the expansion of comic book and paperback fiction publishing.[8] Nevertheless, many elements of the dramatic and garish heritage of the 'classic' pulps resurfaced after World War II. A new era in pulp publishing was heralded in 1937 by the launch of Fawcett Publications' *True* magazine. In its sensational accounts of 'real-life' adventures, *True* represented a new departure in the pulp market; and during the 1940s there followed a growing wave of 'true adventure magazines'. Titles such as *Real* and *Saga* resurrected many of the stylistic codes of the 'classic' era magazines, yet also embodied the preoccupations and fears of post-war America in the way that they constructed a coarse, hard-boiled and aggressively heterosexual masculine universe (see Figure 1).

Gender and sexual identity were ideological battlefields in America throughout the post-war era. In her comprehensive study of American domesticity during the 1940s and 1950s, Elaine Tyler May demonstrates the close relationship between the nation's foreign and domestic policies, showing how pressures for social and sexual stability intensified as non-conformity – whether in political, social or sexual terms – was perceived as a threat to American security.[9] In this strategy of 'domestic containment', marriage and home-making were presented as bulwarks against the spread of Communism, academics, politicians and the mass media all rallying behind the suburban nuclear family as the mainstay of American liberty. In the realm of popular culture, television series such as *Ozzie and Harriet* (1952–66), *Father Knows Best* (1954–63) and *Leave It to Beaver* (1957–63) depicted an idealised family life of bliss and contentment,[10] while in the sphere of social science, Talcott Parsons championed the nuclear family as the mainstay of social stability.[11]

The impact of the post-war idealisation of domesticity on the lives of American women has been the focus of considerable historical scholarship. Feminist critics such as Wini Breines[12] and Stephanie Coontz[13] have pointed to the way in which a battery of popular cultural texts and academic discourse (especially within the emerging sphere of child development) combined in an attempt to convince women that the role of housewife and mother was natural and fulfilling – and that to step beyond these normative roles was in some way abnormal, even deviant. This dominant ideal

Figure 1: *Saga*, 15:2 (November1957)

of domestic femininity found its counterpart in an equally powerful ideology of masculine domesticity, which promoted the hardworking corporate employee and content suburban husband as the ideals of American manhood. This form of masculine identity was distinguished by what Barbara Ehrenreich terms the 'breadwinner ethic' – a form of adult masculinity that promulgated ideals of sober conformity and self-restraint in which men denied themselves in order to provide for their wives and families.[14] During the early 1950s, Ehrenreich argues, 'there was the firm expectation ... that required men to grow up, marry and support their wives. To do anything else was less than grown up, and the man who wilfully deviated was judged to be somehow "less than a man".'[15]

The expectation that men should conform to the role of loyal employee and responsible father registered strongly in popular texts of the period. *Life* magazine's declaration of 1954 as 'the year of the domestication of the American Man' was echoed by the representations of happy suburban fatherhood in television sitcoms, while Steven Cohan shows graphically how the white, middle-class breadwinner was a central fixture of Hollywood films throughout the 1950s.[16] The 'breadwinner ethic' was also endorsed by a weight of academic opinion. Following the lead of Talcott Parsons, Morris Zelditch emphasised the importance of the nuclear family and firmly demarcated gender roles, arguing that 'the American male, by definition, must "provide" for his family... His primary area of performance is the occupational role, in which his status fundamentally inheres; and his primary function in the family is to supply an "income", to be the "breadwinner".'[17] The man who failed to conform to the 'breadwinner ethic', therefore, was deemed either morally or ideologically suspect. Here, then, concerns about the vitality of American fatherhood merged with wider anxieties about masculine identities as homosexuality was incorporated into the McCarthyite demonology of spectres threatening the security of the USA.[18] Indeed, as Ehrenreich observes, in both the psychiatric literature and popular culture of the period 'the image of the irresponsible male blurred into the shadowy figure of the homosexual'.[19]

During the post-war era, therefore, the figure of the white, middle-class, domestic-oriented man emerged as a hegemonic ideological construct obscuring the profound social and economic divisions that remained central to American life. Instead, the 'breadwinner ethic' fostered an impression of unity, cohesion and social stability. These dominant articulations of masculine identity were, however, always more vulnerable and problematic than their omnipresence might have suggested. As Cohan demonstrates, many of the 1950s' most popular films registered a sense of insecurity and doubt around the figure of the 'breadwinner', an unease that stemmed from a set of highly charged changes in American sexuality and lifestyle that seemed to herald a developing 'crisis of masculinity'.[20]

The 1950s were a period of paradoxes, inconsistencies and contradictions, underlined by the publication, in 1948 and 1953, of the Kinsey reports into American sexual behaviour. Sharply at odds with publicly espoused norms of probity, fidelity and heterosexuality, Kinsey's findings pointed to a vast, clandestine world of sexual experience. In particular, Kinsey's widely circulated work undermined hegemonic representations of masculinity by revealing that not only had a surprising number of men had homosexual encounters and relationships, but that female sexuality peaked late in life while male virility seemed to wane much earlier. Alongside confident representations of contented and fulfilled breadwinners, then, there also developed a sense of deep anxiety about the condition of American masculinity, a mood captured in 1958 by *Look* magazine's series of probing articles under the banner 'The Decline of the American Male'.[21]

Above all, it was corporate conformism and the grip of domesticity that were cited as the blight of American masculinity. The title of Sloan Wilson's novel, *The Man in the Gray Flannel Suit*, provided an enduring emblem for the bland miasma of white-collar complacency and domestic drudgery that many saw as the affliction of American manhood.[22] In his best-seller, *The Lonely Crowd*, David Reisman epitomised this stance.[23] For Reisman, the rise of conformity amounted to a kind of emasculation, post-war America seeing the rise of an 'other-directed' man who followed blindly the lead of those around him in a desperate search to 'belong'. In a similar vein, business journalist William Whyte's study, *The Organization Man*, lamented the passing of rugged individualism and the rise of a white-collar world that rewarded conformity rather than initiative, crushing the individual beneath the collective will of the organisation.[24] In various ways, authors such as C. Wright Mills,[25] Daniel Bell[26] and Vance Packard[27] all echoed these anxieties, elaborating critiques of a culture that they saw as suffocating individuality and freedom beneath a blanket of authoritarian uniformity.[28] In these terms, the button-down conformity of the grey-flannel breadwinner came to resemble the decidedly un-American ethos of oppressive 'totalitarianism'.

However, in the context of the Cold War it was not easy to criticise the institutions of corporate America. As both Ehrernreich[29] and Gail Dines[30] argue, critics found a more acceptable target in the figure of the American woman. More than corporate capitalism, it was American women who were routinely cited by authors, academics and journalists as the bane of American manhood. Possibly the most mysogynistic version of the thesis was delivered by Philip Wylie in *Generation of Vipers*.[31] First published in 1942, this book sold so well that it had reached its twentieth pressing by 1955. Coining the term 'momism', Wylie lambasted mothers for smothering their sons with over-affection and overprotection, turning them into passive and effete weaklings.[32] Wylie continued his tirade against the 'womanization of America' throughout the 1950s, accusing women not only of debilitating the American male within the confines of the home, but also of increasingly undermining and displacing him within the spheres of business and the arts.[33]

Despite its prevalence, therefore, the 'breadwinner' ethos was never a monolithic and uncontested ideological force. However, the strongest critiques came not from socially progressive voices of dissent and resistance, but from misogynist reactionaries such as Wylie. In the realm of popular culture, Wylie's rear-guard action against the 'decline' of American masculinity was paralleled by the creed of the macho pulps. Throughout the 1950s and early 1960s, magazines like *Action for Men*, *Man's Life*, *Man's Magazine*, *Men*, *Man's Adventure*, *Man's Illustrated*, *Man to Man*, *Man's World* and *Man's Daring* offered escape into a world of bravado, adventure and dangerous exploits. The titles of these macho pulps rang out their glorification of a hairy-chested machismo, their pages revelling in a celebration of hard-bitten manfulness. Like Wylie, the macho pulps fell over themselves to affirm a ruggedly virile masculine identity in the face of a perceived 'feminisation' of American manhood. Indeed, in an editorial that could almost have come from Wylie's pen, *True* magazine announced to its readers that it aimed to 'stimulate the masculine ego at a time when man wants to fight back against women's efforts to usurp his traditional role as head of family'.[34]

TRUE ADVENTURES FOR BOLD MEN

During the 1950s and early 1960s, the macho pulp market was dominated by a relatively small coterie of publishers (Magazine Management and Emtee were two of the major players). The circulation of individual magazines, moreover, was not huge – usually hovering at a figure of around 100,000–200,000.[35] However, the sheer volume of titles ensured that the macho pulps were a publishing phenomenon of some significance, and as late as 1967 even their competitors conceded that the genre had a total circulation of around 12,000,000 a month, with a net sales revenue of up to $1,500,000.[36]

Breathless accounts of combat, warfare and feats of staggering bravery or endurance were the staple ingredients of the macho pulps. The magazines' dramatic covers commonly featured muscle-bound and granite-jawed GIs as either the intrepid heroes of daring suicide missions or the courageous saviours of imperilled (and usually semi-naked) women (see Figure 2) Inside, the stories and features offered similar fare. The battles and skirmishes of World War II were remorselessly recounted and re-fought. Typical stories appearing in the December 1960 edition of *Man's Life* magazine included 'Escape from the Nazi Head-Hunters' ('I was stranded in the heart of Nazi country – capture would be worse than death') and 'Last Chance to Skip Hell' ('Our battered ship didn't merit a Jap torpedo, but this hulk

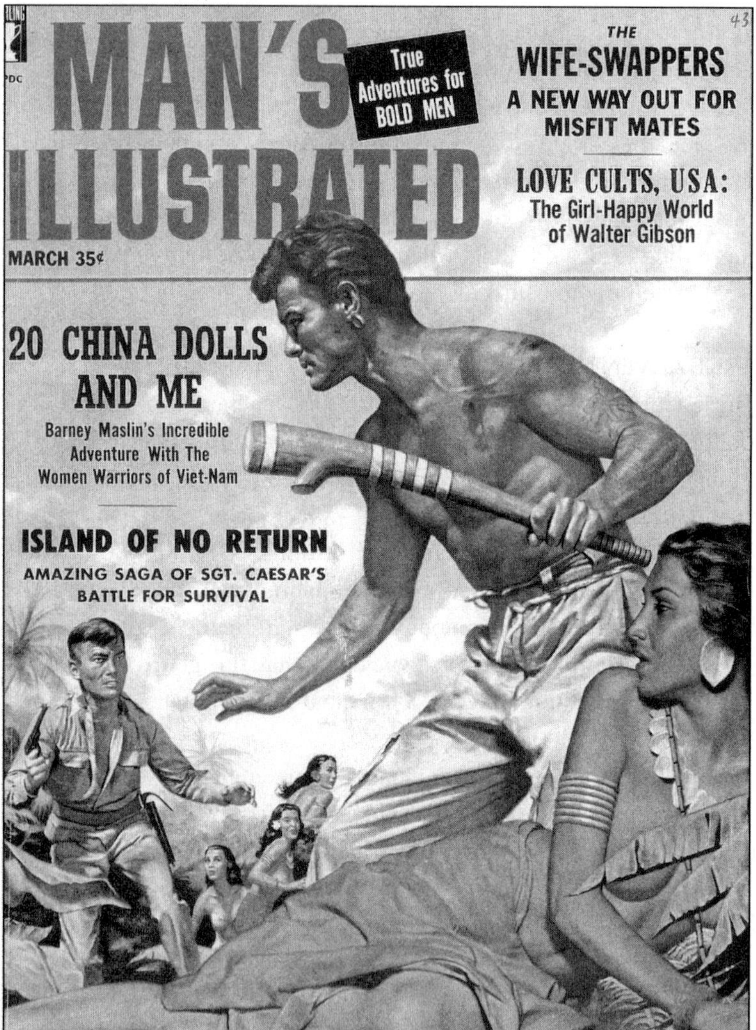

Figure 2: *Man's Illustrated*, 4:9 (March 1959)

had to save our lives'). Authors were zealous and inventive in their creation of 'true' accounts of 'blood 'n' guts' action, Mario Puzo (author of *The Godfather*) recalling how, as a macho pulp writer, he gleefully 'created a whole new battle for Berlin... There were only 6000 casualties on D-Day, but in my battles there were hundreds of thousands. In a way, I'm prouder of those battle stories than my other writing. They required greater imagination.'[37]

In their tales of death-defying action, the racism and xenophobia of the macho pulps became glaringly apparent. The magazines' heroes were, without exception, wholesome white Americans or (occasionally) western Europeans. With the growing sensitivity of civil rights issues, the macho pulps seldom depicted their villains as recognisably black, yet (partly, perhaps, as surrogates) the magazines declared open season on German and Japanese soldiers, as well as a motley assortment of Arab Sheikhs, Asians and Aborigines. These ethnic villains were depicted as archetypes of bestial cruelty. Japanese and Nazi officers were routinely shown as perpetrators of cowardly atrocities against allied troops or – more frequently – as the grinning torturers and abusers of beautiful white women (see Figure 3) Not untypical were stories such as *Men Today*'s 'The Doomed Harlots in Hitler's House of Horror' (November 1963) and *Man's Life*'s 'Run From the Rape Beasts of Hanoi' (December 1968).

In a curious observation, Gail Dines contends that the macho pulp genre offered 'an escapism founded on danger and adventure rather than sex'.[38] In reality, however, sex came to rival violent combat as the magazines' chief obsession. The sexual objectification of women was central to the way in which the macho pulps constructed a notion of dominant and aggressively heterosexual masculinity. Their covers invariably featured stylised illustrations of semi-naked and sexually alluring young women, while no magazine was complete without its 'glamour' section of 'cheesecake' photo-spreads. The same preoccupation surfaced in the pulps' advertising sections – with promotions for an array of 'Classic Stag Films', 'Brazenly Frank Photos' and erotic lingerie from catalogues such as 'The Undi World of Lili St. Cyr'. A kind of

Figure 3: *Men Today*, 6:4 (July 1966)

prurient 'sexual tourism' was also a trademark of the macho pulps, with regular features on the sex capitals of America and the wider world. In 1952, for example, *Men* magazine focused on 'Frisco – Gateway to Sin' (March) and 'Sin on Top of the World: The Shameful Story of Anchorage, Alaska' (June). Similarly, *Male* revealed 'One Block of Vice' in New York (October 1950); *Man's Magazine* highlighted Nevada as America's 'Sin State', where 'men are men and women are available' (February 1960); and *Stag* featured 'Paris' Once-A-Year Wild Free-Love Blast' (January 1967). Usually, salacious titillation was thinly disguised as a 'public service' exposé, yet occasionally all pretence to righteous social concern was abandoned as a magazine got carried away with lustful fantasies of easy sex – as in *True Adventure*'s account of life in Mexico where 'You can live on a shoestring, love on a dime in these unspoiled, untamed border towns, where chicks come a peso a parcel and a leer can get you a lot more than a lire' (April 1964).

A striking duality was central to the macho pulps' representation of women. On the one hand they were fascinated with strong, aggressive and sexually assertive forms of femininity. Often, this would appear in stories of 'exotic' women making insatiable sexual demands on helpless men, for example, *Sir!* magazine's Polynesian tale of 'Duke Moore's 3 Years as a Stud Slave' (February 1961) or *Man to Man*'s account of imprisonment in a 'Stud Farm on a Heavensent Island' ('Henri was tossed into the barred cage and the native women struggled at the door to be the first to get inside' (September 1961) (see Figure 4). A similar theme also surfaced in stories of nubile saboteurs and commandos dealing destruction and death to the Axis powers, for example, 'The Fantastic Vengeance of Norway's Sub-Sinking Joy Girls' (*Men Today*, November 1963) or 'The Wild Assault of Scott's Bazooka Blondes' (*Real Combat Stories*, August 1966). Alongside these fantasies of a rapacious and predatory femininity, however, the covers, stories and features of the macho pulps habitually featured sexual violence, torture and torment of the grossest kind. In the universe of the macho pulps, women were routinely whipped, burned, drowned, assaulted and murdered (see Figure 5). This duality, then, suggests a sense of

Figure 4: *Sir!*, 17:6 (February 1961)

masculinity being under siege. The macho pulps were both fascinated by, and enormously fearful of, women's sexuality. In an age of apparently profound changes in gender relations and sexual behaviour, these magazines sought to 'put women back in their place', to regain a position of uncontested dominance for traditional American manhood.

These anxieties also lurked behind the macho pulps' obsession with self-improvement and personal advancement. Nagging doubts about employment, physique and sexual virility made themselves felt throughout the magazines. Above all, these insecurities surfaced in the advertising content. Largely aimed at blue-collar workers and servicemen, it is unsurprising to find advertisements for jobs and training courses in their pages. Yet their tone could verge on the paranoiac, denoting a desperate search for status, security and success: 'How to Speak and Write Like a College Graduate', 'Meat Cutting Offers *You* Success and Security' or (from a car insurance firm) 'Compare This *Interesting Job* to the One You Have Now'. Fears of physical imperfection and deficiency also figured prominently, with a plethora of advertisements for girdles ('Now – Look Younger, Feel Younger, More Attractive – With Amazing New Man Power Figure Belt!'), hair restorer ('Starting to Get Bald? Take Hope For New Hair With Brandenfel's Home System!') and body-building courses ('Don't Spend Your Life on the Sidelines Watching Big Brawny He-Men Grab the Most Attention, the Best Jobs, The Prettiest Girls!'). Above all, the American male's sense of inadequacy seemed to register most strongly in the bedroom, the macho pulps featuring a battery of advertisements for sex guides and manuals ('Marriage. The Happiest Day of Her Life – and the Most Tragic! Because They Did Not Know the Latest Facts About Sex Revealed in This Amazing Book!').

The preoccupations and anxieties of the macho-pulps reveal an American masculinity characterised by deep feelings of insecurity. They testify to a sense of traditional manhood assailed by social and cultural change and desperately trying to establish a sense of power over social roles and gender relationships that seemed to be increasingly beyond its control. In these terms, the macho pulps

Figure 5: *Men Today*, 6:3 (May 1966)

were undoubtedly conservative and highly reactionary, a right-wing extremism that became especially visible in their rabid hatred of Communism and 'murderous reds'.[39]

At the same time, however, it would be misleading to see the macho pulps as unitary texts, unproblematically reproducing dominant ideologies. Popular texts are seldom this philosophically coherent. As Tony Bennett and Janet Woollacott have argued eloquently, popular culture is shot through with contradictions and is a site 'around which a constantly varying and always many faceted range of cultural and ideological transactions are conducted'.[40] Indeed, Joel Foreman shows insightfully that, for all their elements of conservatism, many of the mass-media representations of the 1950s played 'a significant role in the dismantling of very powerful and regressive mores and systems of belief',[41] although in the macho pulps it is hard to identify many spaces for subversion and radical appropriation. Admittedly, it may have been possible for their representations of the spectacle of the male body to be co-opted by a homoerotic gaze. Yet, overall, what remains enduringly striking is their reactionary elements of racism and misogyny. Certainly, the macho pulps were 'subversive' in the way they challenged hegemonic ideologies of masculinity. In their celebration of muscular manhood and their penchant for salacious sleaze, they contested the bourgeois ideal of the domesticated, grey-flannel breadwinner. Yet they did so from a position of belligerent reaction, mirroring Joseph McCarthy's rampant hatred of 'egg-sucking phoney liberals', who, with their 'pitiful squealing', held 'sacrosanct those Communists and queers' in the American government who were betraying American interests.[42] The world of the macho pulps was clearly at odds with post-war bourgeois ideals of probity, rectitude and domesticity – but rather than being emancipatory or progressive, their 'resistance' was violently reactionary.

THE FINAL SHOWDOWN FOR THE MACHO PULPS

During the late 1950s, cracks increasingly appeared in the hegemony of the grey-flannel breadwinner. The greatest challenge to this brand of bourgeois masculinity, however, came not from the swaggering butchness exemplified by the macho pulps, but from a sybaritic celebration of consumption embodied in the mythology of the playboy. Antithetical to consumerism and hedonistic leisure, the breadwinner ethic was increasingly out of step with the pace and trajectory of social and economic change. By the mid-1950s, the ethos of hard work, moderation and decorum associated with the breadwinner and the 'organisation man' was becoming anathema to a form of capitalism that increasingly prioritised consumption, hedonism and immediate gratification. In place of the breadwinner, Ehrenreich argues that American manhood increasingly aspired to the ideal of the playboy – a masculine ethos that refused to succumb to the fetters of domesticity and instead prioritised a quest for personal gratification in a swinging world of endless leisure, luxury and indulgence.[43] The playboy ethos, therefore, performed an adaptive function on behalf of the dominant order, providing an avenue through which American men began to explore the widening horizons of conspicuous consumption, unabashed pleasure-seeking and less inhibited forms of (hetero)sexual expression.

The playboy was already emerging in nascent form in inter-war America, manifested in the launch of *Esquire* as a stylish fashion and 'lifestyle' magazine in 1933. Yet it was during the late 1950s and early 1960s that the playboy credo came into its own. In the field of magazine publishing, an early hint that change was afoot came in 1951 with the launch of *Modern Man*. Aping the style of *Esquire*, *Modern Man* combined 'glamour' pictorials with general fiction and 'lifestyle' features. Yet *Modern Man* also owed a debt to the macho pulps. It appealed to the 'action man' rather than the 'leisure man' through features that were red-blooded, robust and resolutely 'manly': 'How to Run a Submarine' (May 1952), 'Hickok – Hell's Own Marshall' (July 1954). More than *Modern Man*, it was Hugh Hefner's *Playboy* magazine that articulated most successfully the mythology of the laid-back and lavishly hedonistic American bachelor.

Launched in 1953, *Playboy* was an immediate publishing success. It's first print-run of 70,000 copies virtually sold out, circulation soaring to a million a month by 1956 and rocketing to over four million by 1967. As several critics have noted, the secret

Figure 6: *Cavalier*, 5:46 (April 1957) (a)

Figure 6: *Cavalier*, 13:119 (May 1963) (b)

of *Playboy*'s success lay in the way it combined sex and status, winning a mainstream distribution and readership by carefully integrating pornography within the context of an up-market lifestyle magazine.[44] The success of *Playboy* inspired a host of imitators, for example *Gent* (launched in 1956), *The Dude* (1956), *Hi Life* (1958), *Bachelor* (1959) and *Millionaire* (1964), all eulogising the playboy ethic of pleasure, narcissism and conspicuous consumption. The rough-and-ready world of the macho pulps was increasingly outmoded by changes in American masculine identities, and magazines that did not adapt would go to the wall.

Several titles chose to throw in their lot with the playboys. *Cavalier*, for example, had been a fairly standard macho pulp in the early 1950s, with its emphasis squarely on 'action and adventure for men'. By the early 1960s, however, it had successfully restyled itself as an Epicurean lifestyle magazine, luxuriating in a world of stylish chic, fine food and drink, foreign travel and 'tasteful' erotica (see Figure 6). Other titles chose a 'downward' option. *Wildcat*, for example, made nude pictorials a more central feature of its content, thereby relocating itself more fully in the 'mainstream' pornography market. Titles such as *Man's Daring* and *World of Men* took another course: their covers, stories and illustrations became increasingly sensational, lurid and bizarre, mirroring the rise of 'exploitation' magazines and tabloids (see Figure 7)

Although magazines such as *Action For Men*, *Man's Life*, *Stag* and *Battle Cry* survived until the late 1960s, by this time the sun had set on the world of the macho pulps. Their brand of gritty, blood 'n' guts machismo in the great outdoors had been out-paced by changes in American masculine identities. From the mid-1950s, there began to emerge a dominant masculine ethic that rejected the shackles of domesticity, yet which also eschewed the robustly macho world of the 'action man' in favour of a hedonistic universe of leisure and conspicuous consumption. The hegemony of the grey-flannel breadwinner, therefore, was ultimately undermined not by blood 'n' guts machismo but by the lounge suit and the dry martini.

Figure 7: *Men's Daring*, 4:2 (November 1962)

Notes

1. Philip Wylie, *Generation of Vipers* (London, Frederick Muller, 1955), p. 216.
2. Though the term 'macho pulp' did not have currency during the post-war decades, it is a term I use to denote a genre of cheap men's magazines marked out by their common form, style and content.
3. P. Biskind, *Seeing Is Believing: How Hollywood Taught Us to Stop Worrying and Love the Fifties* (New York, Pantheon, 1983).
4. Lary May (ed.), *Recasting America: Culture and Politics in the Age of the Cold War* (Chicago, Chicago University Press, 1989).
5. Joanne Meyerowitz (ed.), *Not June Cleaver: Women and Gender in Postwar America, 1945–1960* (Philadelphia, Temple University Press, 1994).
6. Jeffrey Weeks, *Sexuality and Its Discontents: Meanings, Myths and Modern Sexualities*, (London, Routledge, 1985), p. 44; and *Sex Politics and Society: The Regulation of Sexuality Since 1800*, 2nd edn (London, Longman, 1989), p. 254
7. More extensive accounts of the way in which women were encouraged (and sometimes forced) to leave the world of work and return to the domestic fold can be found in M. Allen, 'The Domestic Ideal and the Mobilization of Womanpower in World War II', *Women's Studies International Forum*, 6:4 (1983), pp. 401–2; K. Anderson, *Wartime Women: Sex Roles, Family Relations and the Status of Women During World War II* (Westport, Greenwood Press, 1981); and S. Hartman, *American Women in the 1940s: The Home Front and Beyond* (Boston, Twayne, 1982).
8. Authoritative accounts of the rise and decline of the 'classic' era pulp magazines can be found in B. Blackbeard, 'The Pulps', in M. Thomas Inge (ed.), *Handbook of American Popular Culture*, Vol. I (Westport, Greenwood, 1978), pp. 195–223; R. Goulart, *Cheap Thrills: An Informal History of the Pulp Magazines* (New Rochelle, Arlington House, 1972); F.M. Robinson and L. Davidson, *Pulp Culture: The Art of Fiction Magazines* (Portland, Collector's Press, 1998); and L. Server, *Danger Is My Business: An Illustrated History of the Fabulous Pulp Magazines: 1896–1953* (San Francisco, Chronicle, 1993).
9. Elaine Tyler May, *Homeward Bound: American Families in the Cold War Era* (New York, Basic Books, 1988).
10. For a more detailed discussion of the way in which American television popularised and celebrated ideals of suburban domesticity after World War II, see M Haraloich, 'Sitcoms and

Suburbs: Positioning the 1950s Homemaker', in L. Spigel and D. Mann (eds), *Private Screenings: Television and the Female Consumer* (Minneapolis, University of Minnesota Press, 1992), pp. 111–43; L. Spigel, *Make Room for TV: Television and the Family Ideal in Postwar America* (Chicago, University of Chicago Press, 1992); E. Taylor, *Prime-Time Families: Television Culture in Postwar America* (Los Angeles, University of California Press, 1989); and T. Weisblat, 'What Ozzie Did for a Living', *The Velvet Light Trap*, 33 (Spring 1994), pp. 14–23.

11. Talcott Parsons, 'The Social Structure of the Family', in R. Anshen (ed.), *The Family: Its functions and Destiny* (New York, Harper Row, 1949), pp. 241–73; and 'The American Family: Its Relation to Personality and the Social Structure', in T. Parsons and R.F. Bales (eds), *Family, Socialization and the Interaction Process* (Glencoe, Free Press, 1955), pp. 3–33.
12. Wini Breines, 'Domineering Mothers in the 1950s: Image and Reality', *Women's Studies International Forum*, 8:6 (1985), pp. 601–8; and *Young, White and Miserable: Growing Up Female in the Fifties* (Boston, Beacon Press, 1992).
13. Stephanie Coontz, *The Way We Never Were: American Families and the Nostalgia Trap* (New York, Basic Books, 1992).
14. Barbara Ehrernreich, *The Hearts of Men: American Dreams and the Flight From Commitment* (London, Pluto, 1983), pp. 11–12.
15. Ibid.
16. Steve Cohan, *Masked Men: Masculinity and the Movies in the Fifties* (Bloomington, University of Indiana Press, 1997).
17. Morris Zelditch, 'Role Differentiation in the Nuclear Family: A Comparative Study', in T. Parsons and R.F. Bales (eds), *Family, Socialization and the Interaction Process* (Glencoe, Free Press, 1955), pp. 307–51.
18. John D'Emilio provides an incisive analysis of the way in which the rhetoric of the Cold War fused fears of Communism with anxieties about homosexuality and sexual identity: *Sexual Politics, Sexual Communities: The Making of a Homosexual Minority in the United States, 1940–1970* (Chicago, University of Chicago Press, 1983); and 'The Homosexual Menace: The Politics of Sexuality in Cold War America', in K. Peiss and C. Simmons (eds), *Passion and Power: Sexuality in History* (Philadelphia, Temple University Press, 1989), pp. 225–40. See also J. D'Emilio and E.B. Freedman, *Intimate Matters: A History of Sexuality in America*, 2nd edn (Chicago, University of Chicago Press, 1997); D. Savran, *Communists, Cowboys and Queers: the Politics of Masculinity in the*

Work of Arthur Miller and Tennessee Williams (Minneapolis, University of Minnesota Press, 1992); and A. Sinfield, 'Un-American Activities', in A. Sinfield, *Cultural Politics – Queer Reading* (London, Routledge, 1994), pp. 40–59.

19. Ehrernreich, *The Hearts of Men*, p. 24.
20. Cohan, *Masked Men*.
21. In the same year, *Look* magazine republished the articles in book form as *The Decline of the American Male* (New York, Random House, 1958).
22. Sloan Wilson, *The Man in the Gray Flannel Suit* (New York, Simon and Schuster, 1955).
23. David Reisman, *The Lonely Crowd* (New Haven, Yale University Press, 1950).
24. William Whyte, *The Organization Man* (New York, Simon & Schuster, 1956).
25. C. Wright Mills, *White Collar: The American Middle Classes* (New York, Oxford University Press, 1951).
26. Daniel Bell, *The End of Ideology: On the Exhaustion of Political Ideas in the Fifties* (New York, Free Press, 1960).
27. Vance Packard, *The Hidden Persuaders* (Harmondsworth, UK, Penguin, 1960); and *The Status Seekers: An Exploration of Class Behaviour in America* (London, Longmans, 1960).
28. Richard Pells, *The Liberal Mind in a Conservative Age: American Intellectuals in the 1940s and 1950s* (New York, Harper Row, 1985) is a useful overview of liberal intellectual critiques of 'conformity' in post-war American culture.
29. Barbara Ehrernreich, *The Hearts of Men*, p. 36.
30. Gail Dines, 'Dirty Business and the Mainstreaming of Pornography', in G. Dines, R. Jensen and A. Russo (eds), *Pornography: The Production and Consumption of Inequality* (London, Routledge, 1998), pp. 37–64.
31. Philip Wylie, *Generation of Vipers* (London, Frederick Muller, 1955).
32. For more detailed analyses of the notion of 'momism' and fears of domineering motherhood in post-war America, see Breines, 'Domineering Mothers in the 1950s: Image and Reality'; and L. Fisher, 'Mama's Boy: Filial Hysteria in *White Heat*', in S. Cohan and I. Hark (eds), *Screening the Male: Exploring Masculinities in Hollywood Cinema* (London, Routledge, 1993), pp. 70–84.
33. Philip Wylie, 'The Abdicating Male: And How the Gray Flannel Mind Exploits Him Through His Women', *Playboy*, 3:11 (November 1956), pp. 23–4 and 50; and 'The Womanization of

America', *Playboy*, 5:9 (September 1958).

34. Cited in M. Brenton, *The American Male* (London, George Allen and Unwin, 1967), p. 30.
35. For example, typical average circulation figures were *Man's Conquest*, 164 000; *Man's Illustrated*, 177 000; and *Man's Magazine*, 200 000 (source: *Ulrich's On-Disc Record* (London, R.R. Bowker, 1998). The bulk of this circulation was based on news-stand sales rather than subscriptions.
36. F. Mullally, 'Adults Only?', *Penthouse*, 2:12 (1967), pp. 20–24.
37. Quoted in T. Weyr, *Reaching for Paradise: The Playboy Vision of America* (New York, Times, 1978), p. 5.
38. Gail Dines, 'Dirty Business and the Mainstreaming of Pornography', p. 45.
39. On occasion, the shrill anti-Communism of the macho pulps could become almost farcical, as when *Sir!* magazine asked 'Are Nudist Camps Communism's Newest Strong-Hold?' (April 1951).
40. Tony Bennett and Janet Woollacot, *Bond and Beyond: The Political Career of a Popular Hero* (Basingstoke, UK, Macmillan, 1987), p. 8.
41. Joel Foreman (ed.) *The Other Fifties: Interrogating Midcentury American Icons* (Chicago, University of Illinois Press, 1997), p. 21.
42. Quoted in S. Wittner, *Cold War America: From Hiroshima to Watergate* (New York, Praeger, 1974), p.95.
43. Ehrernreich, *The Hearts of Men*, p. 41.
44. Gail Dines, '"I Buy It For the Articles": *Playboy* Magazine and the Sexualization of Consumerism', in G. Dines and J.M. Humez (eds), *Gender, Race and Class in Media: A Text-Reader* (London, Sage, 1995), p. 55; Gail Dines, 'Dirty Business and the Mainstreaming of Pornography', p. 45; and B. McNair, *Mediated Sex: Pornography and Postmodern Culture* (London, Arnold, 1996), p. 112.

CHAPTER NINE

Containing Batman: rereading Fredric Wertham and the comics of the 1950s

Will Brooker

Batman is a text, an icon, a template open to a potential infinity of readings. He has run the gamut from the all-American Japanazi-slapper of 1943 and the paunchy clown of the 1966 television series to such diverse forms as a science-fiction adventurer, a war-bond salesman, a pop art artefact and a tortured intellectual. The most contentious reading, however, suggested that Batman's sexuality might be open to question. In his study of the Batman comics, *Seduction of the Innocent*, Dr Fredric Wertham concluded that the relationship between Batman and Robin was a homoerotic one.[1] Wertham based his observation upon the testimonies of 'overt homosexuals' being treated at the 'Quaker Emergency Service Readjustment Center,' who had drawn their own fantasies from the pages of Batman comics:

> At home they lead an idyllic life. They are Bruce Wayne and 'Dick' Grayson. Bruce Wayne is described as a 'socialite' and the official relationship is that Dick is Bruce's ward. They live in sumptuous quarters, with beautiful flowers in large vases, and have a butler, Alfred. Bruce is sometimes shown in a dressing gown. As they sit by the fireplace the young boy sometimes worries about his partner ... it is like a wish dream of two homosexuals living together.[2]

What this chapter seeks to do is re-examine Wertham's take on Batman more closely than usual. It will also refer to the comic texts and to some of the intertextual frames that might have governed the

1954 reading, which we must remember was not dreamed up by some crackpot doctor in isolation but was put to Wertham by gay readers of the period, no matter that they were in the Quaker Emergency Service Readjustment Center at the time. I will suggest that Wertham's campaign against comic books was part of a wider discourse of containment that sought to categorise and isolate potential threats to the precarious status quo of post-war America. By referring to texts of the period, this chapter aims to demonstrate that comic books and homosexual behaviour were subject to parallel discourses that identified them as 'social problems' and discussed their corruptive 'effects' in similar terms. Wertham's *Seduction of the Innocent*, from its title onwards, tapped into these twin discourses of panic around 'delinquency' and 'deviancy', and achieved much of its considerable impact by tying two existing concerns into a single cultural form, within a contemporary societal discourse of containment of which McCarthy's crusade against Communism was simply the most notorious example.

WERTHAM IN CONTEXT: 'DEVIANCY' AND COMIC BOOKS IN THE 1950S

Andy Medhurst says of Wertham that he 'writes with anguished concern about the potential harm that Batman might do to vulnerable children, innocents who might be turned into deviants'. I hesitate to say that Medhurst is wrong, but his is not my reading of Wertham. What Wertham actually says is this:

> Many adolescents go through periods of vague fears that they might be homosexual. Such fears may become a source of great mental anguish and these boys usually have no one in whom they feel they can confide ... during and after comic-book reading they indulged in fantasies which became seriously repressed. Life experiences, either those drawing attention to the great taboo on homosexuality or just the opposite – experiences providing any kind of temptation – raise feelings of doubt, guilt, shame and sexual malorientation.[3]

We might quibble with the term 'malorientation' (which, after all, is very 1954), but overall, rather than expressing shock and outrage,

Wertham's tone seems one of quite reasonable concern. Rather than advocating a witch-hunt against deviants, he understands that in a climate where homosexuality is a great taboo, gay fantasies might be a source of worry for young men. However clumsy his attempts to help these boys, his project actually seems a misguided liberal one, its flaws tied up with his cultural context rather than stemming from any kind of personal bigotry; indeed, much of Wertham's crusade against 1950s comics is based on their crude representation of women and black characters. His obvious hatred of racism in particular suggests a man whose views, for the time, were in fact on the progressive side. Although Wertham's passage about Bruce, Dick and their dressing gowns is clearly heavy-handed, his overall suggestion, at the beginning of his discussion on Batman, is merely that 'a subtle atmosphere of homoeroticism' pervades the comic; not a scenario of 'deviance' but, in his own words, a 'love-relationship'. It is very easy, as Andy Medhurst proves, to set Wertham up as an Aunt Sally and deride him from a cultural position some thirty-five years later; but to gain a more accurate perspective we have to consider the cultural framework in which Wertham was operating.

As noted above, *Seduction of the Innocent* fell within a wider social project of categorisation and containment that sought to identify, isolate and examine potential threats to the social body of America with the aim of either curing them or cutting them out completely. Kinsey's vast enquiry into sexual behaviour is part of this culture of classification, even if its attitude towards homosexuality was more liberal than many of the psychological studies of the gay 'problem' that followed it. The McCarthyite hunt for Communists shares the same project of obsessive identification and categorisation. In turn, the investigations into the 'juvenile delinquent' in which Wertham played a part echo this need to pigeonhole and isolate problematic members of society. While homosexuality, Communism and delinquency may seem to present very different social 'problems', the discourses surrounding them in the early 1950s were remarkably similar and were frequently conflated. James Gilbert writes in *A Cycle of Outrage* that popular fears in the 1950s were centred around a 'predominant metaphor ... of contagion, contamination, and infection. In some senses, these were the interchangeable parts of a larger political and social dialogue during the 1950s. An invasion from the outside, from beyond the family, the community, the group, or the nation threatened treasured institutions.'[4]

As an illustration, Gilbert quotes Senator Hendrickson, addressing the June Conference on delinquency in the year *Seduction of the Innocent* was published: 'Not even the Communist conspiracy could devise a more effective way to demoralize, disrupt, confuse and destroy our future citizens than apathy on the part of adult Americans to the scourge known as Juvenile Delinquency.'[5]

We need only to compare the articles on comic books from 1952 to 1955 with those on 'Sex Perversion' – as the *Reader's Guide* for those years terms homosexuality – to see that parallel discourses were in operation. Between 1953 and 1954, *Newsweek* spoke of a 'Delicate Problem',[6] *Time* of a 'Hidden Problem'[7] and 'Unspeakable Crime'.[8] During the same period, *Changing Times* warned against 'Dirt and Trash',[9] the *English Journal* discussed a 'challenge' to society,[10] and *Time* was alarmed at 'Horror on the Newstands'.[11] The former refer to homosexuality, the latter to comics, but the same images of threat and illicit deviance resound through both. Homosexuality is a 'problem', comics are a 'challenge'. Homosexuality is a 'crime', comics are a 'horror'. Wertham's own article in the *Ladies Home Journal*, 'What Parents Don't Know', only compounds the parallels; the phrase could quite easily refer to a son or daughter being gay, rather than to the danger of comic books.[12]

The echoes between these discourses on comics and deviancy can be traced back well into the 1940s. In February 1946, for example, the State Education Department surveyed the 'effects' of comic books on children, concluding that many parents would be 'shocked and horrified' if they knew the books' content. A 'youth forum' on WQXR radio in 1945 asked boys and girls what they thought of comic books, to which one boy responded that 'bad books' were 'immoral', and that 'many of them give a distorted picture of things'. A priest who claimed to have surveyed 10 000 young people on the subject warned of the 'perils' that comics posed to children.[13]

In March 1948, a symposium at the New York Academy of Medicine, entitled 'The Psychopathology of Comic Books', condemned comics for 'stirring primitive impulses that retarded the development of socially desirable behavior and attitudes'.[14] Towards the end of the decade, the National Congress of Parents and Teachers were supporting 'decency crusades' against comics, while the editor of the *National Education Association Journal* described the comic industry as threatening 'indecency ... the perversion of the child mind'.[15]

'Immoral', 'indecency', 'distorted', 'primitive', 'retarded', 'shocked and horrified', 'influence on youth', 'perversion': all these key words and phrases could equally be found in discussion of homosexuality during the 1940s and early 1950s, the period of Wertham's primary campaign. Most studies of the period, including those of the American Medical Association, regarded homosexuality as a disorder suitable for psychiatric treatment, although others advocated shock therapy and hormone replacement to redress a genetic 'vulnerability'.[16] Brown and Kempton's *Sex Questions and Answers* of 1950 provides the characteristic overview that 'in dealing with this problem ... a complete "cure" is still very rare',[17] while even more liberal studies proposed that homosexuality may be 'better than isolation ... or it may be an added destructive touch in a deteriorating personality'.[18]

Wertham may have been the first to draw concerns about the 'deviant' and the 'delinquent' social type so explicitly together, then, but in doing so he only made clear a link that was already implicit within the overarching discourse of social 'problems' and their 'treatment'.[19] That apparently separate moral concerns could very easily be called to serve under a wider banner is indicated by the quotation from Hendrickson (above) and had, in any case, already been demonstrated four years previous to the publication of *Seduction of the Innocent*, when Senator Joe McCarthy pledged to purge the Government of not just Communists, but 'queers',[20] and proceeded, to much public acclaim, to weed out both suspected Reds and supposed homosexuals in the State Department for interrogation.

The harassment and persecution of suspected homosexuals under McCarthy's crusade – and the extent, as a partial consequence, of institutionalised homophobia throughout the 1950s –parallels closely the more notorious anti-Communist witch-hunts and legislation. Ninety-one employees were dismissed on the grounds of alleged 'sex perversion' in 1950 alone, not one of them daring to appeal. Within the military, the penalty for 'homosexual acts and tendencies' was a dishonourable, 'blue' discharge, which stigmatised the bearer for life and barred him from all benefits promised in the GI Bill of Rights.[21] In the workplace, almost all employment agencies refused to take on 'effeminate' men, and stamped 'a number or a letter on their applications that means "gay", and virtually unplaceable'.[22] Indeed, homosexuality was technically a sex crime in many states, punishable by indeterminate and involuntary hospitalisation in a mental institution: as Thomas Szasz notes in Marmor's *Sexual Inversion*, the fact that gay men were rarely incarcerated solely because of their sexual conduct 'does not alter the intent of the legislation or its potential threat'.[23]

The US government's policy of the time was outlined clearly in a document entitled 'Homosexuals and other Sex Perverts', and offered a key to spotting homosexuals through effeminacy and 'a dislike for women'.[24] Psychiatrists compounded this received notion by explaining to young men that 'Homosexuals didn't become doctors; they became hairdressers, interior designers, that sort of thing.'[25] Many gay men who grew up in the 1940s or 1950s internalised these crude stereotypes to the extent that they were unable to identify themselves as homosexual, or alternatively retained their cover by explicitly avoiding such codes. As Howard Brown explains in his memoir, *Familiar Faces, Hidden Lives*, 'being seen with a hairdresser'[26] or discussing 'such otherwise taboo topics as cooking'[27] were enough to make a man appear suspect. Brown confesses, 'I was afraid of revealing my homosexuality by showing the slightest interest in color schemes and the like.'[28]

We might note, as an aside, that 1957 saw a story called 'The Rainbow Batman' in which Bruce Wayne proudly displays an entire wardrobe of costumes in pumpkin-orange, lime and canary-yellow, as well as the usual dull grey and blue. 'I must, Robin – I must wear a different-colored Batman costume each night!' Batman proclaims, fastening his cloak. Although Robin describes this as the red outfit, the cape and trunks Batman has chosen are clearly magenta and the bodysuit is a pale pink.[29]

In the context of a 1950s America, where covert homosexuality was identified by gays and straights alike through a variety of subtle clues, Wertham's reading of a 'love-relationship' and 'subtle atmosphere of homoeroticism' through certain visual signifiers does not seem as ludicrous or as reprehensible. At the very least, it must be pointed out that Wertham took the trouble to examine the Batman comics of the 1950s himself and attempted to perform, however clumsily, the same kind of textual reading that he believed his patients had opened up. Few of his critics have ever matched this diligence in research.

Admittedly, Batman comics of the early 1950s are rather harder to come by now than they were forty years ago, but they can be found, and they make suggestive reading. In story after story, Batman and Robin clearly exhibit a love and trust for each other that extends beyond the generic conventions of the adventure or science fiction narrative and into the domestic sphere, providing ample material to support the relationship described by Wertham and the boys whose testimonies informed his reading.

Take, as just one instance, 'The Man Who Stole the Joker's Jokes', a story from 1951.[30] The narrative opens with Bruce and Dick at home in Wayne Manor, reclining on the sofa. Bruce is indeed wearing a gown as he reads the newspaper and Dick watches the television. The scene speaks of a relaxed, intimate bonding between two men. 'What do you say we go out and see the fair in person, Dick?' Bruce asks. 'A wonderful idea – let's go,' exclaims Dick, and they're off. Five pages on and the demands of the crime genre have kicked in, as the Joker catches Robin in the fairground Tunnel of Love and Batman is seen in close-up, rubbing his chin in concern. 'Robin is gone! This is serious … he never disobeys an order! Something must have happened to him!' In the next scene, Commissioner Gordon receives a ransom note. He and Batman appear in mid-shot in the police office. 'What are you going to do?' asks Gordon. Batman looks away, fist clenched in a melodramatic pose. 'The only thing I can do – surrender! I'd do anything for that kid!' This explicit declaration of commitment, even devotion, is compounded by the next two panels, which again invoke the conventions of melodrama. Robin is shown in the foreground of his prison, with crooks jeering him as he weeps. The next frame depicts Batman in long shot, pacing the cave with his shadow thrown before him, as the caption describes 'a distraught and lonely figure'.

It hardly takes a reading 'against the grain' to see this as a depiction of tenderness and compassion between two men. Indeed, the storytelling comes intriguingly close to the conventions of the romance comic. Batman and Robin are often framed together in tight close-up, with the emphasis on distraught facial expression and emotion instead of action. Even the perfectly-shaped tears on Robin's cheeks call to mind the weeping girls that Lichtenstein picked out from the pages of heterosexual romance titles, rather than the thundering cannons and screaming fighter planes of his war canvases. This story does not, of course, demonstrate that Batman and Robin have a gay relationship any more than it demonstrates that they live as a surrogate father and son, or are simply platonic colleagues. It does, however, demonstrate the hooks in the stories of the early 1950s upon which a gay teenager could readily hang his own reading.

At a pinch, the very motifs of the superhero lifestyle can be read as tallying with the experience of being gay, particularly in the 1950s. This exercise was carried out at length by a recent article in *Gay Times*, which noted that Batman and his colleagues:

> … all lead dual lives. If they do reveal their alternative personae to anyone … it is usually to their closest friends and their family. They fight a continual battle against prejudice … some support the underdog. The parallels with gay experience go further. Superman and a majority of the X-Men were born with their

> mutant powers ... but many don't realise they possess such powers until they reach their early teens. Some try to resist the change and deny the urge. Others (take the Boy Wonder for example) embrace the new culture and lifestyle with relish, creating gaudy, vivid apparel and an arrogant attitude.[31]

The article is credited to Megan Radclyffe, a name that has, to my ears, the air of a gaudy, invented superhero title about it. But superhero names are important: we should remember that the Mattachine 'homophile' association of the 1950s was built around fanciful pseudonyms and passwords, and that Donald Cory, the author of the pioneering study, *The Homosexual In America*, felt the need to publish, and republish twenty years later, under a false name for fear of repercussions. The practice of prominent gay men disguising their identity when writing on homosexuality continued far into the 1970s. On a quotidian level, the memoirs of gay men such as Howard Brown testify that giving false names was standard practice in the bars of the 1950s, and that 'gay', dropped into casual conversation, figured as a secret code and sign of recognition. Finally, we might consider in turn that both 'Bruce' and 'Wayne' were widely considered to have 'gay' overtones after the 1950s. E. Nelson Bridwell, the commentator who huffed at that 'certain psychiatrist', lamented in 1971 that 'today, when a comedian calls someone Bruce, you can almost bet he means the guy is a swishy character'.[32] It was for this precise reason that Bruce Banner, aka The Hulk, was renamed David in the 1977 television series; Bruce just wasn't a Hulky enough name.

'Society has handed me a mask to wear,' wrote Donald Cory in *Homosexuality*, 'a ukase that it shall never be lifted except in the presence of those who hide with me behind its protective shadows. Everywhere I go, at all times and before all sections of society, I pretend.'[33] The motif of double lives, and the constant fear of exposure that this entailed, is paramount in the testimonies of gay men who passed as straight during the 1950s. When we look from these testimonies to the Batman comics of the period it becomes striking how often the theme of hidden identity recurs. On the surface, Batman's secret is his alter ego as Bruce Wayne; but it is not hard to imagine that this repeated motif could have acquired a personal resonance for a young man having to hide his sexuality in the early 1950s. Again, a few examples should furnish the context.

Howard Brown reports, for instance, that in 1956 he turned down a promotion for fear of discovery by his prospective boss: 'The thought of Mr and Mrs Jacobsen coming by while I was giving a gay party or merely sitting at home with a lover was chilling. If they, or some other straight couple, did not realize I was gay the first time they popped in, they surely would the second.'[34] The consequences of such a discovery were horrific, with every potential to wreck a man's career, undermine his social reputation and poison his relationship with his friends and family. Brown relates the story of Henry, forced to resign from the Air Force when he was accused of being gay; the fact that his address book contained no women's names was all the 'proof' needed.[35] Henry was subsequently refused membership of the American College of Surgeons when his sexuality was rediscovered, on the grounds of 'poor moral character'.[36] We also hear of Lloyd, ordered to resign after a private investigator hired by his employers interrogated neighbours until they revealed that he lived with a man;[37] and of Daniel, a gay teenager who was brutally ostracised within his small Midwest town and eventually banished by his parents.[38] Of himself, Brown concludes, 'I had lived for a long time with the fear of being "discovered". Every homosexual has lived with this fear.'[39]

With this in mind, consider *Batman*, 182 (April 1951), in which the Puppet Master threatens to reveal Wayne's face beneath the mask – 'Now the climax of the show! The unmasking of Batman!' – and *Detective*, 188 (October 1952), in which Batman warns Robin that if Wayne Manor is destroyed, 'our identities will be revealed'. It seems entirely possible that for a young man like Daniel, such stories might have struck a chord. And the parallels would surely be made explicit by *Detective*, 194 (April 1953), which opens with a revelation – a document stating plainly that 'Bruce Wayne is the Batman!' – and develops into a tense drama based solely around Batman's desperate attempt to keep his hidden life concealed. At the climax, a criminal in possession of the vital document taunts

Batman with the ultimate threat – 'I'll tell the world who you really are!' – and Batman gulps, 'H-he knows my secret!' The suspense of the moment is stressed in a caption: 'Is this the end of Batman's secret identity? Is his secret about to be revealed to the world?' Reassurance comes only when we learn that the document was written in invisible ink, and the villain holds nothing but a blank sheet of paper.

While the motif of hidden identity and discovery obviously takes on a stylised, adventure-serial form here, it nevertheless seems hardly surprising that the boys interviewed by Wertham, their own lives dominated by the very real fear of discovery and its consequences, should have found some appeal and even solace in Batman's fantasy world of intense paranoia coupled with regular sighs of relief. After all, the hero's identity always remains intact, and his sidekick is always returned to him for an embrace in the final frame.[40]

The histories of men who related their experiences of discovering their sexuality in the 1940s and 1950s are not unlike the experiences of those Batman fans or indeed, to stretch the point, of Batman and Robin themselves: their testimonies are characterised by double lives, secret relationships, platonic infatuations, unspoken love and frequent self-doubt. To take just one example from *Growing Up Before Stonewall*, Ed, who was nineteen when *Seduction of the Innocent* was first published, talks of his 'very mixed feelings about physical pleasure coupled with psychological anxieties... I was annoyed and confused ... it was difficult thinking that I might be a true homosexual. I probably tried to rationalise it away, or was just very confused about it.'[41]

Howard Brown confirms that 'years-long contemplation of suicide is typical of many homosexuals who discovered their sexual identity in the 1940s and 1950s. I know that during my college years, whenever I heard that someone had committed suicide, my first thought was: I wonder if he was homosexual.'[42] Again, in this light, Wertham's concern for the 'great mental anguish' of the boys he interviewed does not seem quite so ridiculous or as narrow-minded.

'Proof', like 'truth', is a dirty word in the cultural studies I come from; but a final piece of evidence serves my argument well. This is an article called 'Batman and Robin Made Me Gay'. It is an autobiographical piece by a gay man, the late Steve Beery, from *Gay Comix* (September 1986). Beery was 'a kid in the early '60s', but crucially, the comics he read were 'reprints from the 1940s and '50s' – precisely those that Wertham and his patients were studying. His testimony below bears this out, both in his engagement with the detail of Wayne Manor's furnishings and in his emotional investment with the duo's relationship:

> Some kids wanted to be Batman. I wanted to be Robin. Batman was the Daddy: accomplished, perfect, remote. Robin was just like me, only more so ... he got to live in an elegant mansion with sumptuous furnishings and a butler. In the secret Batcave deep beneath the house, he worked out, wrestled and studied crime detection. He drove his own Batcycle and flew his own Whirlybat. Best of all, he had the undivided loyalty of Batman.

Beery speaks of the 'bond that linked the two partners', evident in the 'situations where Robin's life was in jeopardy', and makes plain the 'romantic' nature of his identification. Most significantly, he explains that this long-term romantic drama could be read beneath and beyond the cyclical, episodic crime-and-punishment stories.

> For all the emphasis on detection, on puzzling over clues and chasing the crazy villains, the Batman and Robin stories were about devotion – to their crime-fighting ideal and, more importantly, to each other. Unwittingly, and to my undying gratitude, Batman and Robin made me gay.[43]

Beery, of course, was reading the reprints. Had he grown up in the 1950s with the originals, his response might have led him into 'readjustment', rather than to San Francisco. Those ten years made a lot of difference. Yet, although a reader like Beery might never forgive Wertham's course of action, even by situating it within the very different context of the early 1950s, his every word suggests that he would find no fault with Wertham's detection.[44]

The homoerotic aspects of Batman about which Wertham showed such concern in the 1950s have been embraced by some gay fans in the 1990s as a framework for their own experiences and indeed fantasies. This chapter will end with a further indication of this, in the form of an *Attitude* feature that asked readers to confess their childhood crushes on television characters. Andy, aged thirty, says of Burt Ward and Adam West, 'I thought Batman was really hunky ... and fatherly ... but I also liked Robin for being cute and boyish. Sometimes I'd fantasise about being one of them, fancying the other one; other times I'd swap round; sometimes I even imagined being a third party in the relationship.'[45] It is striking how vividly this echoes the testimony in *Seduction of the Innocent* of the boy who confesses 'I think I put myself in the position of Robin. I did want to have relations with Batman ... I felt I'd like to be loved by someone like Batman.'[46]

From a sad, touching psychological case study to a jokily embarrassed column in a national gay magazine, the climate has changed but the reading is identical. It is my belief that Wertham, had he lived to read Andy's testimony, would have applauded the circumstances that made such a relaxed confession possible, and would have seen no reason to interfere.

Notes

1. Fredric Wertham, *Seduction of the Innocent* (London, Museum Press, 1955). It should be noted here that Wertham was not the first to see a homoerotic relationship between Batman and Robin. *Seduction of the Innocent* was prompted by the earlier research ('several years ago') of a 'Californian psychiatrist' (p. 190). Although Wertham is frequently accused of inventing or creating the notion of a 'gay Batman', he in fact made an interpretation visible that had previously been hidden and repressed. In stressing this potential level of meaning in the Batman text, despite his project of censorship, Wertham actually highlighted and disseminated this queer reading, which has since permeated even the most mainstream of Batman texts as well as informing aspects of 1990s 'gay culture'.
2. Wertham, *Seduction of the Innocent.* This reading has been somewhat divisive. 'Wertham,' says Paul Sassienie, 'deliberately,

or otherwise, missed the point, that in truth Bruce Wayne and Dick Grayson's relationship was no more than that of father and son.' [Paul Sassienie, *The Comic Book* (London, Ebury Press, 1994), p. 58.] Reinhold Reitberger calls Wertham's interpretation 'a libellous propaganda campaign' and stresses that 'Batman has now sent teenage-wonder Robin to college where he seems to show a normal and lively interest in the opposite sex.' [Reinhold Reitberger and Wolfgang Fuchs, *Comics: Anatomy of a Mass Medium* (London, Studio Vista, 1972), p. 123.] E. Nelson Bridwell bristles at 'a certain psychiatrist [who] decided that a man and boy living together spelled homosexuality,' calling it 'one of the most irresponsible slurs ever cast upon our heroes.' [E. Nelson Bridwell, *Batman From The 30s To The 70s* (New York, Crown Publishers, 1971), p. 12.] Mark Cotta Vaz cites the opinion that 'if they had been actual men, they could have won a libel suit' and concludes 'it was sad that Wertham got so much mileage out of his unwarranted attacks on Batman. This was the same Batman who had fought Nazi spies and aided the War Bond effort.' [Mark Cotta Vaz, *Tales of the Dark Knight: Batman's First Fifty Years 1939–1989* (London, Futura, 1989), p. 47.] Andy Medhurst brands Wertham a 'crazed' homophobe with a project of 'shrill witch-hunting'. He quotes that infamous paragraph and responds: 'To avoid being thought queer by Wertham, Bruce and Dick should have done the following: never show concern if the other is hurt, live in a shack, have only ugly flowers in small vases, never share a couch, keep your collar buttoned-up, keep your jacket on and never, ever, wear a dressing-gown.' [Andy Medhurst, 'Batman, Deviance and Camp', in Roberta E. Pearson and William Uricchio, *The Many Lives of the Batman* (London, Routledge, 1991), p. 151.] In a remarkable echo of Medhurst's retort, Freya Johnson, in an article on the 'queer supratext' of Batman Forever picks out the same passage and comes up with the same reply: 'Obviously they must be fags: otherwise they'd have a butler named 'Butch', live in cramped quarters littered with beer-cans, wouldn't show concern for one another's injuries or be caught dead in a dressing-gown and cultivate only (what?) cactuses in small ugly metal pots?' [Freya Johnson, '"Holy Homosexuality Batman": Camp and Corporate Capitalism in "Batman Forever"', *Bad Subjects*, 23 (December 1995), http://english-server.hss.cmu.edu/bs/23/johnson.html.] I find it intriguing that a single paragraph can both incense the nervously homophobic fan-boys as a queer slur on their hero and the queer theorists as a homophobic slur on gay identity. This contradiction alone, I think, warrants a closer look at the texts that many of these commentators seem never to have read: that is, Wertham's original four pages, and the comics he studied.

3. Wertham, *Seduction of the Innocent*, p. 189.
4. James Gilbert, *A Cycle of Outrage: America's Reaction to the Juvenile Delinquent in the 1950s* (New York, Oxford University Press, 1986), p. 75.
5. Ibid.
6. 'Delicate Problem', *Newsweek*, 43 (1954).
7. 'Hidden Problem', *Time*, 62 (December 1953).
8. 'Unspeakable Crime', *Time*, 61 (November 1953).
9. 'Dirt and Trash that Kids are Reading', *Changing Times*, 8 (November 1954).
10. 'Comic Books, a Challenge', *English Journal*, 41 (December 1952).
11. 'Horror on the Newstands', *Time*, 64 (September 1954).
12. Wertham, 'What Parents Don't Know About Comic Books', *Ladies Home Journal*, 70 (November 1953).
13. *New York Times* (14 February 1946; 16 December 1945; 24 August 1946).
14. Amy Kiste Nyberg, *Seal of Approval: The History of the Comics Code* (Jackson, University Press of Mississippi, 1998), p. 32.
15. Ibid. p. 37.
16. Quoted in Judd Marmor (ed.), *Sexual Inversion* (New York,Basic Books, 1965), p. 6.
17. Quoted in Donald W. Cory, *The Homosexual in America* (New York, Paperback Library Inc, 1951), p. 186.
18. Dr Clara Thompson, quoted in Cory, *The Homosexual in America*, p. 191.
19. See also Michel Foucault, *Discipline and Punish* (London, Allen Lane, 1977).
20. Robert Griffiths, *The Politics of Fear: Joseph R. McCarthy and the Senate* (Lexington, University Press of Kentucky, 1970), p. 89.
21. Cory, *The Homosexual in America*, p. 44.
22. Howard Brown, *Familiar Faces, Hidden Lives: The Story of Homosexual Men in America Today* (New York, Harvest, 1977), p. 163.
23. Thomas Szasz, 'Legal and Moral Aspects of Homosexuality' in Marmor, *Sexual Inversion*.

24. Cory, *The Homosexual in America*, Appendices.
25. Brown, *Familiar Faces, Hidden Lives*, p. 35.
26. Ibid. p. 51.
27. Ibid. p 10.
28. Ibid. p. 148.
29. Sheldon Moldoff, 'The Rainbow Batman!', *Detective Comics*, 241 (March 1957).
30. 'The Man Who Stole The Joker's Jokes', *Batman*, 67 (1951).
31. Megan Radclyffe, 'Comics 'r' Us', *Gay Times* (November 1996).
32. Bridwell, *Batman From The 30s To The 70s*, p. 12.
33. Cory, *The Homosexual in America*, p. 11.
34. Brown, *Familiar Faces, Hidden Lives*, p. 144.
35. Ibid. p. 152.
36. Ibid. p. 154.
37. Ibid. p. 152.
38. Ibid. p. 90.
39. Ibid. p. 4.
40. To talk of 'gay experience', a 'gay lifestyle' or even 'gay culture' is of course contentious, and some can get away with it more easily than others. Andy Medhurst's real problem with Wertham, it sometimes seems, is not that he identified aspects of 'gayness' in the Batman text but that he did it from 'outside' the culture: that Wertham was straight. As a straight man myself, I am aware that the same criticism could be levelled at me; but I would contend that when attempting to reconstruct the cultural context of the 1950s, most of us are obliged – whatever our sexual preferences – to rely on secondary texts rather than our own personal histories. I did not live as a gay man in 1954, but neither did Andy Medhurst, who was born at the end of that decade. However, Howard Brown did, and Donald Cory did, and so did the subjects of *Growing Up Before Stonewall: Life Stories of Some Gay Men*; (n. 41); the testimonies of all these gay men echo strongly the views of Fredric Wertham as well as the parallels suggested by Megan Radclyffe.
41. Peter M. Nardi, David Sanders and Judd Marmor (eds), *Growing Up Before Stonewall: Life Stories of Some Gay Men* (London, Routledge, 1994), p. 116.
42. Brown, *Familiar Faces, Hidden Lives*, p. 41.
43. Steve Beery, 'One Reader's Story: Holy Hormones! Batman and Robin Made Me Gay!', *Gay Comix*, 8 (Summer 1986). Thanks to Randall Scott of the Michigan State University Library Special Collection.

44. In the 200-odd pages of Martin Barker's influential study of 1950s comic censorship, *A Haunt of Fears*, there are only four lines on Wertham's interpretation of Batman. *Seduction of the Innocent*, says Barker dismissively, 'repeats the old story about the homosexual relations between Batman and Robin ... apparently some of Wertham's patients got quite a thrill from imagining this relationship!' Martin Barker, *A Haunt of Fears* (London, Pluto Press, 1984), p. 68.
45. Murray Healy, 'Turned In, Turned On', *Attitude* (January 1997).
46. Wertham, *Seduction of the Innocent*, p. 192.

CHAPTER TEN

Romance and history: Anya Seton's *The Winthrop Woman*

Julie Hughes

> This book is built upon a solid framework of facts; from these facts I have never knowingly deviated, nor changed a date or circumstance. My determination to present authentic history has necessitated a scrupulous adherence to the findings of research ... (m)ine has been the job of re-creation and interpretation, 'putting the flesh on the bones'.[1]

In early 1958, Houghton-Mifflin published Anya Seton's *The Winthrop Woman*. It was chosen as the *New York Times Book Review*'s book of the month for March. It was the story of Elizabeth Fones, niece of John Winthrop, the first Governor of the Bay Colony in the opening chapter of American history. Written by an already established author, Seton's novel was hailed as her new best-seller and her publishers ran an initial 'passionate advertising campaign of 20,000 unpuritanical dollars'.[2] According to Alice Hackett's figures in her best-seller lists,[3] *The Winthrop Woman* sold over four million copies in its first year and rates as the fourteenth highest selling novel in the period 1950–59. This figure, however, highly underrepresented the actual copies produced and sold as it is based upon hardback copies sold through trade outlets – bookstores and libraries – and does not include the expanding paperback distribution or book clubs. The novel featured in the *Publisher's Weekly* best-seller list from March until mid-September. In spite of this best-selling status, I have found only one critic who discusses *The Winthrop Woman*, and this is a reductive reading.[4] This chapter will argue that Seton's novel extends the genre's function to that of criticism – a criticism cushioned somewhat by allegory and made palatable for a female readership, but one that nevertheless undermines the Cold War narratives of history and nationhood precisely because of its subject and context.

Historical fiction was an established best-selling genre, and the historical romance was a popular woman's genre. The publication of Seton's best-selling historical romance novels spans a thirty-year period from 1941 to 1975. Her books are the types to be found in both the large-print and regular sections of public libraries. Most second-hand dealers stock some of her thirteen titles; some lovingly have whole sections dedicated to her work. Charity shops and boot sales also prove fertile grounds. Generations of women have read her novels, both in America and Britain, and she is considered by the fans of this genre to be possibly the best of her generation.[5] As a consequence, she has consistently been a massively popular best-selling author.

Seton's framing device of an opening 'Authors Note' and closing 'Historical Afterword'[6] confirm this impulse and function to question the discreteness of the categories of history, fiction and biography as Seton's preferred title of historical biographer illustrates. This, of course, could be interpreted as an authorial movement away from the romance category, as historical fiction tends to be taken more seriously than the historical romance. My preferred term for Seton's work, therefore, would be a historical writer who adopts some of the conventions of the romance genre, if only to subvert them. In a novel the length of *The Winthrop Woman* (574 pages), the pursuit-of-true-love plot would inevitably wane if it were the only plot. Seton spent more time researching her longer books than most of us spend writing a Ph.D. thesis.[7] Educated at Cambridge, she used her researching skills to cover meticulously every angle of her chosen subject's life. In writing the biography/novel of a woman who existed in an historical period pivotal to American history, and calling herself a biographer, she is in fact rewriting the history of great men and, by implication, the history of America. As a reader and maker of cultural history, her narrative impulse rescues the figure of the silent woman in history from the margins, and retrospectively orders the past. As the reconstruction of Puritan history, which had begun in the 1930s, was built upon the biographies of famous men, this may be read as a critique of how gendered Cold War narratives of history and nationhood were written in the 1950s.

The history of Puritanism had been that of an elite, written by an elite, concerned with the history of ideas. Professional historical scholarship in the post-war period had stressed objectivity and the commitment to search out and report the 'truth' of the past. This, it was claimed, could be achieved only through a sharp distinction between, 'the knower and the known, between fact and fiction, and above all, between history and fiction'.[8] Complexity and relativism were viewed with distrust and the attempt was made to trivialise this approach to history by linking it to cynicism and nihilism, thereby making it over as un-American.[9] The figure of Seton as historical researcher explodes this allegiance to historical objectivity as she willingly declares that, 'This book is built upon a solid framework of fact; from these facts I have never knowingly deviated, nor changed a date nor circumstance. I have hoped that readers would be interested in following the story as it emerged *for me* in the original documents.'[10]

Using historical facts as they emerged *for her* again complicates how to define this book: a problem I ascribe to the slippage between the categories of history, fiction and biography that Seton's work inhabits happily. The author's note commonly used by Seton acts as a declaration of her own theories of historical truth. She sees her role as that of *rewriter* of women's private and public lives and histories, and her literary impulse is the response to both the public and the private silencing of Elizabeth's narrative. As a member of one of America's most famous families, the Winthrops, her cultural significance cannot be underestimated particularly as generations of amateur genealogists had informed a 'biased presentation' that fostered feelings of shame in Elizabeth's descendants. Seton, however, believed that 'Elizabeth's life was significant and praiseworthy'[11] and found evidence that a family member had even gone so far as to mutilate references to her in manuscripts.[12] This acknowledgement of the erasing of women from history parallels the historical limits that women faced in their lives. Seton uses history simply as another narrative in her retelling of Elizabeth's life. Facts are not the only measure of the woman: the original manuscript references to Elizabeth had at times been defaced and altered to fit a specific agenda, thereby already misrepresenting or fictionalising Elizabeth's life.

Impressively, Seton's research records a list of primary sources that any professional historian would have drawn upon, including the five volumes of *The Winthrop Papers* (1498–1649). However, listed as equal in importance are diaries and family letters. Seton not only grants these narratives the same status as those used by 'official' history; she also examines the handwriting techniques of the writers in order to construct her characters. Without ever really examining her own personal value judgements, she declares certain female characters such as Martha, Elizabeth's sister, to have a 'childish scrawl ... and ... pathetic cipher, indicating ... [her] temperament'.[13] The only textual example we are given as readers to compare this statement with is a facsimile of a letter written by Elizabeth to John Winthrop, Jr, her cousin, in 1669. Occupying the page after the title page, Elizabeth's hand-written letter appears to lead the narrative and convey a sense of her writing her own history, perhaps writing herself into history and visibility. To the untrained eye, this letter appears to be scrawled and perhaps an indicator of a weak temperament. However, as Seton's note to the letter points the reader to its place in the body of the novel, the role of the author in reconstructing Elizabeth is heavily evident. This combination of factual document and authorial direction makes no attempt to imply objectivity. In fact, it may even be claimed that in order for Seton's fictional Elizabeth to succeed, all other women in the text are presented as a foil to the eponymous heroine. She has to be *extra*ordinary yet simultaneously typical to fulfil Seton's motive to record the 'emigrant' narrative. Standing for herself, her gender, her family and her nation, Seton claims:

> [Elizabeth was] a woman who suffered the handicaps peculiar to her sex and her time, but she had the remarkable endurance which characterised all the first settlers – those who managed to survive.
>
> This is one reason I have spent nearly four years in research and in writing about Elizabeth. Another reason was the attempt to vilify the founding of New England, and New Netherland days, in terms of a particular family – the Winthrops – and of Elizabeth whose own history is commingled with national affairs.[14]

The figure of the woman Elizabeth and the unconventional life she led disrupts the traditional narrative of history in the retelling. Genderless as a representative of nation her desires may be read as the uncontainable forces that defied the strict Puritan codes and went on to explore and 'tame' the American continent. But as woman, she is not simply relegated to the domestic or, in literary terms, to the realm of the romance. As both nation and woman, history and fiction, Seton's Elizabeth Winthrop presents a troubling figure for history and historiography, one that stresses the *writing* of the past by historians. Seton's work may be seen, therefore, as a rethinking of Cold War historical paradigms, an approach that we would now link to post-modern theories.[15] Seton foresees the epistemological gap in her recognition that the historical labour that has gone on before is mediated and biased. Her retelling or reconstruction illustrates the problem when trying to fit together history (what has been said) and the past (the actual events). In self-reflexively bringing attention to the problems of narrating an event that as historian she can access only through language, Seton as a producer of history bears witness to its very fictionality. Declaring her 'modernisation' of spelling when using original documents illustrates that history is indeed constructed, cleansed and made over through language to fit the intended reading context. As historical fiction works to reconstruct a believable fictional world, it draws very strongly and densely on historical detail, including speech patterns. Character construction is heavily dependent on speech that intimately narrates both the internal and external world of the characters. This apparent verisimilitude acts to confirm the authenticity of the story. The use of modernised, regulated spelling apparently suggests the heavy hand of the teller or the proof-reader, but Seton again overturns this by explaining:

> Seventeenth century spelling was a matter of individual choice or momentary whim. 'Feake' is spelled eleven different ways in the records. I have chosen to spell each name as its owner usually did... The use of 'thee' is baffling; it seems only to have been used privately, and connotes strong emotion except in the case of parents to young children – and it was inconsistent. In Shakespeare, when Petruchio speaks to Katherine he often uses both 'thee' and 'you' to her in the same speech. Margaret Winthrop, in her sweet letters to John the elder, does the same. I have used the second person pronoun sparingly.[16]

Undoubtedly it is the use of archaisms such as those above that add to the historical context, however inaccurate their use may be.[17] On another level, the text is referencing its link to works such as Shakespeare's and drawing upon it to reinforce its authentic nature.[18] The paradox, of course, is that our only records of spoken language are transcripts, always already affected by the processes of history. What Seton is indicating here is the use of literary texts as historical documents or bearers of history. This in itself is interesting in light of literary historiography.

The 1950s witnessed the consolidation and strengthening of New Critical practices in academia. Massively influential, they not only considered the social and the historical to be extrinsic to the study of literature, but they also excluded from their canon and courses any texts or genres that referred to the world outside the text.[19] This can be seen as a wholesale rejection of the social- and material-based criticism of the 1930s. The movement from a sociologically influenced account of literature to the aesthetics of the form reinforced a highly conservative institutionalisation of literature completely divorced from history or politics. Reinforced through textbooks, it presented a theory and canon of American literature that did not have to refer to any cultural context. Its paradigms remained highly influential and its denigration of popular authors' use of the social and the historical as backdrops privileged the aesthetic, the symbolic and the linguistic. This aestheticisation or estrangement of American literature from an American reality monopolised literary study with its emphasis upon white, Anglo-Saxon, Protestant, male authors. The construction of a national American literature divorced from history, following the modernist movement, located the centre of the text in and of itself. It sought to represent not the real, but the forged or counterfeit nature of America. The crisis of representation or meaning rejected the realist form and instead sought out the myth, allegory and fantasy of America, ironically termed the 'romance' by some critics. The result was the creation of the 'eight American authors approach', which monopolised not only those canonised texts, but also the study of those texts.[20] Christopher Lasch has interpreted the discipline of American studies as a propagandist exercise of the 1950s that built upon the core texts or narratives of America in the name of Cold War consensus values. This passion for consensus and obsession with the myth of American-ness reinforced a further split between critical thinking and learning to aid the national purpose. Lasch viewed this as 'a propagation of culture rather than [a] criticism of it'.[21]

The orthodoxy and consensus of historical scholarship also was 'cult-like', according to John Higham.[22] Self-censorship and caution induced by the Cold War climate witnessed a surge of counter-progressive texts that marginalised dissidence. Ideological pluralism sought to report on what had united America and not divided it in its past. The progressive history of the 1920s and 1930s, and the epistemology associated with it, were refuted and revised. Despite this, counter-progressive themes were not unchallenged. In the late 1950s, professional history's objective grip upon its academic and lay audience began to crack. John Higham, writing in 1962, praised the younger generation of collaborative historians who were overhauling the structures of history to stress the ambiguity and plurality of the American past. What he hoped to see for the future were historians adopting the stance of literary critics, such as Lionel Trilling, who viewed America as an ambiguous paradox; liberal in attitude but conservative in behaviour.[23] The more 'liberal' literary critics, such as Leslie Fiedler and Richard Chase, still insisted on the symbolic or mythic uses of history, rather than viewing literature as a social document. These circular literary practices reinforced an estrangement from the non-canonical and constructed an America with a 'limited past'.

In historical scholarship, Perry Miller's *The New England Mind* (1939, 1953), had constructed and mythologised a history of Puritanism with an emphasis on the life of the mind of the Puritan and his theological contribution to American history but not to his social practices. This emphasis upon the intellectual sphere and its legacy upon literature and learning dominated the historiography of Puritanism and the literary criticism influenced by it.

The Winthrop Woman may be seen as a contributor to the new historiography of Puritanism of the late 1950s, a contribution that stresses its subject's ambiguity. Seton declares the influence of scholars such as Miller, and more traditional historical texts. However, more interestingly, her presentation of history as experienced by a woman and narrated by a woman is indebted to letters, diaries and legend. This point emphasises the circular relationship that Seton's work has with its subject. One of the Puritan legacies or contributions to the American way of writing history was the biographical form. Seton's complex use of the biography/novel/romance illustrates that the writing of women's history is inevitably bound up with writing the history of the nation. Such histories are based on far from objective facts, but may actually be based on fictions – fictions in which women's subjectivity was constructed and narrated by men. As the title of the book states, the eponymous heroine is defined through her relationship to the name Winthrop and its men. The Winthrop may refer to her grandfather, husband, uncle or cousin. It may even be taken as a wider reference to her history within Puritanism and the so-called founding of a national character and identity. She is, in fact, a Winthrop only by name for little over a year, yet she is effectively branded so for all of her life. This strategy of naming may be interpreted as a reference to how the history of women had portrayed them in their relationships to men, not as individuals. An entry in a commonplace book of the 1650s stated: 'Womans the centre & lines are men.'[24] Enclosed within the domestic circle, woman's lot was scarcely documented before feminist historians began a reclamatory process to reverse the trend. Seton's emphasis upon the female experience locates the woman at the centre, but simultaneously presents that centre as multifaceted. By extending the domestic metaphor to the local and the national, Seton's fictionalised biography examines the role and position of women in Puritan America and by implication the role and position of the women in the Cold War of the 1950s.

The use of certain conventions of the romance genre allows this comparison. The life goal for women within this trajectory is a fulfilling marriage achieved after a certain degree of courtship, misunderstandings, deferral and denouement. The pursuit of true love plot is characterised by the heroine's attempt to define her own femininity, needs and desires against those of the other characters in the novel. Seton certainly fulfils the second of these conventions, as Elizabeth's beauty (a necessary prerequisite for the romantic heroine) and manners are contrasted with those of the more traditional characters such as Martha, her sister. Unsettling these conventions, however, are the passages in which Elizabeth's femininity is measured against those signs and symbols considered to be pagan and which, within the Cold War context of the 1950s, were perceived to be un-American.

The novel opens in England in 1617, and the seven-year-old protagonist is staring mesmerised at a stained glass window depicting the Virgin Mary as, 'glistening ... like a meadow of dream flowers ... [she] carried a rose in her hand and wore a shining crown... The whole lady shone with light.'[25] This image of womanhood, however, is idolatrous to her father, who despises both its religious and aesthetic purpose. The presence of light linked to a 'feminine' spirituality is also significant in the novel as it functions as a plot device to link the episodes of Elizabeth's growing consciousness. The dour, masculine Puritan religion is contrasted with the enlightening, uplifting pagan festivals of Christmas and

May Day, the Antinomian beliefs of Anne Hutchinson, the spiritual beliefs of the native Americans and the communion with nature that brings ultimate peace to the dying Elizabeth. The use of the historical figure, Anne Hutchinson, is interesting and significant as she was a religious rebel against the Puritan code; her treatment by the Government of the Bay Colony serves to illustrate a strain of intolerance of dissent. Hutchinson's interpretation of the Scriptures and of a benevolent *personal* God is framed in the novel within the discourses of witchcraft by the society that expels her as a 'virago and she-Beelzebub'.[26] Non-adherence to the codes and conventions of the society results in imprisonment and expulsion to an environment that, in Hutchinson's case, resulted in the massacre of her and her family. The extended link between Elizabeth Winthrop and paganism, witchcraft and the native American population is used by Seton to display the ignorance and corrupting powers of the Puritans, as well as, it may be argued, those of Cold War America during the 1950s in which the appearance of conformity to spiritual and secular goals dominated the public psyche.

The narrative of the founding of America, of expansionism and success, is exposed as a cruel totalitarian regime that manipulates the Scriptures to reinforce and perpetuate its ideology. The acquisition of land and the policing of that land and its resources are justified in the name of religion and progress. Seton's position on this issue is complex as Elizabeth also seeks to acquire land as a source both of financial security and to define herself through a sphere that is non-domestic. Blurring the pursuit of love plot, Elizabeth's dream of finding 'freedom – and true love'[27] in the colony is transposed into a love for the land. 'She had never dreamed that it was possible to fall in love with a place... It came to her as a shock – the yearning for possession.'[28] The sexual metaphor is extended into a 'lust' for the land running thick and strong in the blood that emerges as the most enduring relationship in the novel. But she does not reap the rewards of the land purchased from the Siwanoy tribe for twenty-five English coats until the last pages of the novel, in which spiritual revelation and serenity come full-circle and are linked to the episodes of light. In the face of her own mortality, the ecstatic climax is experienced with her friend Telaka,[29] the squaw whose name means twilight and who functions as the go-between linking the realms defined as nature and civilisation, ungodly and godly. The very act of naming the squaw in the novel may be seen as revisionist.[30] In the original historical documents, Seton found evidence of Elizabeth owning a squaw, but she was not named. This act of naming, although inevitably bound up in colonialist terms, does grant a degree of subject-hood to Telaka and the ethnic group she represents. By exposing the selective processes of history yet again, Seton's naming strategy mixes history and fiction as she offers a new reading of the treatment of the Siwanoy tribe. In her research, she in fact found evidence of extreme treatment of the tribe:

> ... since Greenwich is my own home town, and I live on what was once Elizabeth's land. I wish to say here that the virtually unknown 'Strickland Plains' massacre of the Siwanoy Indians by the white men at what is now Cos Cob, Connecticut, seems to have been as shameful and devastating as any massacre – on either side – in our entire American history.[31]

The demonised 'other' in this equation is the civilising processes of the white race and the discourses of history, which have selected certain battles to remember and revere. Warfare, the great equalising experience of the American male, is portrayed as a rite of passage in terms of both gender affirmation and patriotism. Seton adds an interesting slant to this through the ambiguous sexuality of Elizabeth's second husband, Robert Feake. Slight, pale and beardless, he is delicate in appearance, 'his clothes were fresh and spotless. She caught from them a whiff of lavender. He had withdrawn one glove ... she saw that the long sensitive hand was white ... and moreover Feake's fingernails were clean.'[32] The wedding night proves his lack of virility, thus masculinity, as Elizabeth finds herself 'in the role of the teacher'[33] and his subsequent impotence results in Elizabeth's philosophical realisation that she must be mother and not lover to him. His lack of authorial masculinity simultaneously grants Elizabeth the greatest freedom she has ever known, yet traps her socially as he does not appear to the community to be master of his own household. The freedom of this marriage contradicted the religious doctrine that bound women to their husbands.[34] Feake's inability to be a complete husband in a sexual sense is, however, changed temporarily by his enrolment in the reserve armed force. Once in uniform, shouldering a gun, he is 'jerked out of his queerness... In his cuirass, high boots, and red sword-sash of office he looked more manly than she had ever seen him, and she responded with warmth to his embrace.'[35] As readers, we are not fooled by this display, or by Elizabeth's belief in the shallow surface of this masculinity. The sham disintegrates quickly and the inferences of homosexuality return. The climax is the link made between Feake's 'unnatural desires' and the devil. Feake suffers from dreadful nightmares in which he relives an incident in his former life in England. He walks in his sleep and scratches at the walls, calling out the name 'Ralph' over and over again. One night, he attacks a local boy. In the fervour of witch hunting that is sweeping the colony, the boy claims that he saw:

> [A] black man in a cloak, behind our barn, he jumped at me, and held me in his great skinny arms, like he was a hugging me... He kept whispering to me, he was begging me to do – do something. He called me a name like 'Ralph'. I was afeared 'n' struck him. I felt his fingers pressing, burning on my windpipe. I cried out 'n' he let me go.[36]

Unlike the positive links made between ethnicity and light, homosexuality or effeminacy is rooted in references to darkness and later madness. Feake's hero worship of his strong neighbour and friend, Captain Daniel Patrick, allow him to retain the semblance of a 'normal' life. However, when Patrick is killed, Feake kneels beside his dead body and washes his hands in his blood. The action is a 'private revelation', one of almost perverse spiritual significance. The obsessive motions of hand-washing follow this strange reaction. His retreat into an infantile world again reinforces Elizabeth as mother until their attendance at Elizabeth's daughter's wedding propels him into a violent sexual affirmation of his role as husband. The earlier heterosexual rape of Martha by John Winthrop, Jr achieves a beneficial effect in terms of plot device and Winthrop's actions are not questioned. The rape of Elizabeth, however, by her deranged effeminate husband, results in the birth of a deformed child. Feake's 'abnormal' sexual desire is reinforced textually through his inability to 'master' either his wife or himself.

If America is the land of opportunity, then this novel/biography suggests that opportunity is contained and constrained by external factors such as race, class and gender. The narrative of dispossession links Elizabeth to other disenfranchised groups. Their nomadic existence both emphasises their self-reliance whilst simultaneously presenting them as ultimately under the control of higher powers. Within historical paradigms, this is not the vision of America required by the Cold War consensus that sought to illustrate what had united the nation, not divided it. As a narrative of colonialisation, it critiques the expansion of empire and the brutal treatment of dissenters. As almost a third of the novel takes place in England, it may be seen as the denial of American exceptionialism and instead an analysis that examines the links and similarities between Europe and America, links that are both mythic and literal.

In aligning herself to both oral and written histories, Seton makes history accessible for her reader through the dramatisation of national and public events as experienced in women's personal lives. The public and the private are collapsed within the domestic value system as national conflict impacts upon the family, thereby extending the concept of domesticity outside the home. Discontent and contradiction are not contained within this text by the love story narrative. In fact, at closure Elizabeth is dying and her younger husband is seen to be dissatisfied. Pleasure and peace are achieved through a sense of belonging for Elizabeth, belonging not to a man, but to spirituality linked to nature that acts as a critique of the aggressive masculine pursuit of land and colonial expansion. The categories of the social and the subjective, the historical and the literary, the real and symbolic landscapes are collapsed in this book. This may be seen as a revolt against objectivist history and the turn away from history in New Criticism so dominant during the 1950s, as well as a critique of the Cold War period in which women were struggling to define themselves in their ambiguous relation to the domestic realm.

This chapter may be interpreted as a defence of Seton's work in its emphasis upon the historical rather than the romantic elements in her work. This may, of course, be taken as an argument against the romance, or as an attempt to justify it within a more logical, rational structure. However, Seton's narrative irretrievably binds the two strands and the romantic may be read not simply as what women desire but how they attempt to make sense of it. The home and the family are elevated and emotions are central. This act in itself unsettles historical objectivity and its power structures, despite women's exclusion from public power. Presenting a woman behind the Winthrops, we might say behind America, asserts the neglected history of women – a history in which the domestic sphere has operated simultaneously as a source of joy and pain, and one in which women and women's issues are central. However, despite Seton's urge to fill in the gaps, the final words of the book in the 'Historical Afterword' are not for Elizabeth, but for her cousin John Winthrop, Jr – another famous man!

Seton's work is interesting precisely because of its mass popularity during the 1950s and its continued appeal. What is it about her novels that continue to speak to four generations of women? Perhaps they are an indication that, for some, very little has changed in forty years. However, the critical neglect of the romances of the 1950s is indicative not only of a gap in literary history, but also of an uneasiness in approaching the genre in a decade in which women supposedly conformed and were contained by that conformity. The emphasis in the best-selling romances upon women's issues within their traditionally defined gender roles – those of wife, mother and daughter – marked women as essentially different to men. What the romances did not do was to project a singular image of femininity and domesticity. To further complicate this, Seton did not project a singular image of American history.

History may be seen to function for Seton as a vehicle to reorder the past imaginatively, but despite her attempts at inclusion this device also reinforces a concept of America and Cold War American values based upon romantic and bourgeois ideologies of selfhood. The sanitisation of these assumptions is reinforced by Seton's subject choice: *extraordinary* women – women who are already written into history.

The history that Seton presents is both self-enclosed and disturbed by its textual form. If the role of history in the historical romance is perceived as backdrop to the romance plot, then any critique may be absorbed. However, if the romance of history fails to dilute the issues of national identity and nationhood, and these themes are played out through the melodramas of sexual politics, then it is possible to read Seton's historical romances as contradictory challenges to dominant Cold War norms. Nevertheless, it is in the very nature of their contradiction that their conservatism and the reassertion of a holistic mythic past lies, a nature in which the writer need only pad out the flesh of the bones of history and not question this evolution.

Notes

1. Anya Seton, 'Author's Note', in *The Winthrop Woman* (Kent, Coronet Books, 1962).
2. *Publisher's Weekly* (27 January 1958), p. 66.
3. Alice Hackett, *Eighty Years of Bestsellers 1895–1975* (New York, R.R. Bowker, 1977).
4. W. Darby, *Necessary American Fictions. Popular literature of the 1950s* (Ohio, Bowling Green State University Popular Press, 1987). See chapter 7 on the woman's novel or 'weepy'. Kay Mussell discusses *Katherine* (1954) as a romantic biography within 'the domestic mythology of history' in *Fantasy and Reconciliation* (Westport, USA, Greenwood Press, 1984). Kora Caplan and Lillian Robinson mention Seton in passing in reference to other works. In the 1950s, Seton produced four novels: *Foxfire* in 1951, a fictional love story of miscegenation; *Katherine* in 1954, a fictional biography of Katherine Swynford whose descendants went on to win the War of the Roses and so changed the face of history; *The Mistletoe and The Sword* in 1955, again about star-crossed lovers, this time Druid and Roman; and in 1958, her all-time best-seller, *The Winthrop*

Woman, a fictionalised biography of a real figure.

5. L. Henderson (ed.), *Twentieth-Century Romance and Historical Writers* (Chicago, St James Press, 1990). The preface and entry on Seton by Kay Mussell offer an excellent contextualisation of the roots of both the historical and the romance genres.
6. Seton, *The Winthrop Woman*.
7. Dwight Macdonald links this need for extensive research into the culture's pursuit of facts or mania for information: 'The charms of many a best-selling historical novel are not at all to be found inside the heroine's bodice.' [Dwight Macdonald, *Against the American Grain: Essays on the Effects of Mass Culture* (New York, Da Capro Press, Inc., 1983, p. 408.]
8. P. Novick, *That Noble Dream. The 'Objectivity' Question and the American Historical Profession* (Cambridge, Cambridge University Press, 1988), p. 1–2.
9. Ibid. p. 300.
10. Seton, *The Winthrop Woman*, p. 10 (my italics).
11. Seton, *The Winthrop Woman*, p. 7.
12. Also in *Katherine*, Seton stresses how women's histories are prey to the morals of the writers, recorders and scribes of their generation. Of Katherine, 'little was known, except when her life touched the Duke's ... the contemporary chroniclers were mostly hostile ... and in the great historians Katherine apparently excited scant interest, perhaps because they gave little space to the women of the period anyway.' [Anya Seton, 'Author's Note', in *Katherine*, p. 9.] By comparing the author's notes in Seton's earlier novels to those of the 1950s and later, it is possible to trace a distinction between those works that are purely fictional and those that Seton claims as biography. Her first novel, *My Theodosia* (1941), is the story of the daughter of the politician Aaron Burr and their strange obsessive relationship. Theodosia's mysterious death aboard the aptly named vessel, *Patriot*, suggests a closure of sacrifice for women and silencing reconciliation with death. The biographic impulse of *Katherine* and *The Winthrop Woman* was continued into the 1960s with *Devil Water* (1962); however, the historical reconstructions in this novel are families, and as the female protagonist Jenny is based upon less tangible records such as family legend, its status as biography therefore is inaccurate. What is interesting in terms of authorial intention is Seton's brief opening author's note to *Devil Water*. It is much shorter than that of the two other fictionalised biographies, and historical accuracy is confirmed the afterword rather than this opening word. It

appears that some of Seton's readers or critics are less concerned about the historical accuracy of her writing than she had hoped and so she states: 'In my "Afterword" I have given my acknowledgements, some of my sources, a limited biography, and my reasons for drawing certain conclusions. Several people have suggested that I put this material at the *end* of the book, for the information of those who like such data. Many, however, read only for story – and I hope they won't be disappointed.' [Anya Seton, *Devil Water* (London, Coronet Books, 1962), p. 7.] The later novels, *Avalon* (1966) and *Green Darkness* (1972) are entirely fictional and the framing devices are no longer used to authenticate the subject.

13. Seton, *The Winthrop Woman*, p. 13.
14. Seton, *The Winthrop Woman*, p. 14.
15. K. Jenkins, *Re-Thinking History* (London, Routledge, 1991). Jenkins sets up the distinction between history (what has been written about the past) and the past (the event). The new term 'historiography' describes the writing of the past by historians as a method that recognises that the past has come to us as a story or narrative and that the historian cannot go back and check the story against the event. [Jenkins, *Re-Thinking History*, p. 5–6.]
16. Seton, *The Winthrop Woman*, p. 9.
17. An interesting related point to the use of or modernisation of archaic language was the updating of the *King James Version* of the Bible in 1952. Despite being revised in 1901, the *American Standard Version* was never as popular as the *King James Version* completed in 1611. In 1952, the *Revised Standard Version* was welcomed by churchgoers all over America and Canada, sold 2.3 million within its first year, and remained on the best-seller list for the next five years. The main reasons for this updating in the 1950s were stylistic, and in recognition of the progress of Biblical scholarship in the twentieth century. The result was a more 'readable' sanitised Bible, which was easily assimilated into the American way of life, a Bible that had more relevance to the needs of churchgoers. However, it could also be argued that this revision suited the needs of the Cold War culture that demanded consensus and shared values. The teachings of the Bible therefore became more clear-cut and more clearly stated. In a society in which religion was a badge of nationhood and patriotism, church attendance was a signifier of loyalty to God and country. So the adoption of the *Revised Version* can be seen as a test of Americanism, one that was to set the language of worship for the next generation.
18. It is also referring to its Englishness. Seton's father was English, and

her love of English history is evident from the subject matter of her books. Also, it is possible to trace a line of historical inquiry that is investigating the links between America and its colonial past. Seton is not proposing that America is unique or exceptional; rather she is exploring the ties between the old and the new and how both may be criticised.

19. R. Reising, *The Unusable Past. Theory and the Study of American Literature* (London, Methuen, 1986), p. 15.
20. Ibid. p. 20.
21. Christopher Lasch, *The New Radicalism in America, 1889–1963* (New York, Random House. 1967), p. 318.
22. Quoted in Novick, *That Noble Dream*, p.345.
23. John Higham (ed.), *The Reconstruction of American History* (London, Hutchinson, 1962), p. 1–23. This collection of essays was originally produced as a series of radio broadcasts in 1959.
24. L.T. Ulrich, *Good Wives. Image and Reality in the Lives of Women in Northern New England 1650–1750* (New York, Alfred A. Knopf, 1982). This quote is taken from Seaborn Cotton's Commonplace Book, NEHGS.
25. Seton, *The Winthrop Woman*, p. 15.
26. Seton, *The Winthrop Woman*, p. 289.
27. Seton, *The Winthrop Woman*, p. 310.
28. Seton, *The Winthrop Woman*, p. 364.
29. Although a less textually tangible argument, the use of the name 'Twilight' is startling because of its role in lesbian culture. As a metaphor for the shadowy lives that many women led, it is interesting that Seton chooses this name.
30. In *Foxfire*, Seton also deals with attitudes toward the native American peoples and the plight of the mixed-race child. Within ostensibly formulaic romance conventions, she positions a mixed-race courtship and marriage. In itself this is unusual for a popular novel in 1951. The hero's mother is 'a half-breed Indian', [Seton, *Foxfire*, p. 19] the child of a woman abducted from a wagon train who witnessed her family murdered by the Apache Indians. The hero's father was a white history professor who hired the girl as a housekeeper and later married her. Dart, their child, is constructed as a dark, dangerous, mysterious and virile man that the pampered white heroine cannot resist. His dark sexuality is linked stereotypically to his ethnicity, and his intelligence and drive are linked to a white frontier spirit. Closure finds the races and genders more closely aligned. Amanda, the wife, has achieved a degree of independence and self-reliance, whereas Dart has had

the emotional 'rough' edges smoothed away. Despite these romantic conventions, the complex depiction of the lives of the full- and mixed-blood Apache Indians struggling to define their identity is thought-provoking. Images in popular culture of the native American Indian portrayed him or her as a savage, a threat to the economic prosperity and advancement of the white American race, and a sexual threat to the white woman, another material belonging of the white man. The fetishisation of their semi-clad bodies was a staple of low-budget westerns; it was only when clothed and civilised that they could be represented as subordinate side-kicks. Although Seton does fall into the stereotype trap, at times her white characters are displayed as sly and cunning, racist and vicious.

31. Seton, 'Author's Note', in *The Winthrop Woman*, p. 9.
32. Seton, *The Winthrop Woman*, p. 215.
33. Seton, *The Winthrop Woman*, p. 225.
34. Elizabeth's mother, Ann, may be seen as an example of the excesses of how women were bound by the interlocking duties of the church and the marriage bed. Grown old before her time due to continued pregnancies because of her husband's inability to control his sexual desire, she viewed the will of her husband to be as inscrutable as the will of God. As a woman, there was no point in rebellion against either form but 'obedience to it was dreary hard at times'. [Seton, *The Winthrop Woman*, p. 17.] Martha, Elizabeth's sister, is portrayed as being more like their mother and is scared of childbirth. In a bizarre scene, Elizabeth instructs her brother-in-law to forcibly consummate his marriage. This violent consummation/rape finally occurs symbolically on board ship on the voyage to America. The conquering of his wife is linked inevitably to the conquering of the virgin land of America. Ostensibly Martha's dark suicidal tends are 'cured' by the restoration of the normative marital relationship. This in itself is not viewed negatively within the novel; rape within marriage in Martha's case serves only to illustrate Martha's lack of healthy sexual drive. Again she is used as a foil for Elizabeth whose sexuality is a positive factor.
35. Seton, *The Winthrop Woman*, pp. 243–4.
36. Seton, *The Winthrop Woman*, pp. 337.

Considering cultures: how to make sense of our Cold War

Scott Lucas

I write this on the eve of the Senate's trial of the President of the United States for lying about some form of sexual relations with a White House intern. US jets, for the fourth day in a row, have fired missiles at Iraqi air defence emplacements. Simultaneously, it is revealed that United Nations weapons inspectors passed information to US intelligence agencies. The American economy has just grown for the ninety-third consecutive month, and the stock market, led by computer-based shares, is booming. The lead story has little to do with high politics, foreign policy or macroeconomics: apparently, a basketball player named Michael Jordan is to announce his retirement.

However, what strikes me as I sit in this California hotel room is the panoply of images beyond these headlines. There's a documentary about the Chinese community in San Francisco, which ends happily in a combination of tradition and assimilation. You can choose between a satire on New York politics (*Spin City*) and a satire on fashion magazines (*Just Shoot Me*). There's costume jewellery for immediate sale on two different channels. You can watch college basketball, professional ice hockey, or the 'World Championship of Sumo'. On the Fox channel, two young men are competing to set a world record by squirting water from their eyeballs.

There is no coherence here, no focus upon those events which, forty years from now, will be constructed as 'political', 'economic' or 'diplomatic' history. If the polls are right, two-thirds of the populace are bored or unconcerned with the proceedings against Bill Clinton. Only a tiny minority can identify a 'no-fly zone', let alone current trouble spots like Kosovo or Sierra Leone. For most, the dynamics of a global economy mean little apart from the issues of having a job and money in the current account. So, do we take refuge in the standard portrayal of a history implemented by elites – political, financial, technological, military – with the rest of us reduced to a token place in opinion polls?

It is this question that prompts me to consider the prevailing conceptions of the 1950s. Even if life was 'simpler', in the sense that it was pre-satellite and pre-Internet, it was still a period of rapid, unprecedented economic and social change, not to mention the presence of a cold war that was being waged in the era of The Bomb. Yet many historians surveying the period easily reduce it to 'the age of conformity' or 'the golden years'. Surely the power of William O'Neill's conception of an 'American High'[1] or John Patrick Diggins' 'proud decade'[2] lay not in each writer's selective approach towards 'facts' but in the comforting vision of life at home and vigorous defence of policy abroad. Conversely, the inability of I.F. Stone's depiction of *The Haunted Fifties* to become common currency stemmed from the ostracism of Stone who, unlike so-called liberals like Arthur Schlesinger, Jr, did not place his values and his judgement upon the altar of anti-Communism.[3]

One has to go further, however, and challenge the very basis of a history about elites by elites in the service of elites, not through condemnation but through a hard look at the 'rest' of US society. What if apparent complacency or contentment lay not in any embrace of the 'political' or the 'economic' or even a broad 'social' sphere? What if it lay in ignorance or indifference towards any considered coherent conception? I suspect few Americans had any idea where Quemoy or Matsu were, any understanding of the dispute over those islands off the coast of mainland China, or any inkling that the Eisenhower Administration was threatening nuclear war in defence of them. I imagine that only a minority would be cognisant of the issues over work and home raised by *The Man in the Grey Flannel Suit*, and I am certain that David Riesman's celebrated examination of 'inner-directed' and 'other-directed' behaviour did not hold the attention of many. What if my grandmother, Bobbie Lucas of Birmingham, Alabama, spoke for most when asked for her recollection of the civil rights disputes that developed around her in the 1950s, culminating in the famous images of 'German shepherds' and water hoses turned loose on demonstrators in 1963: 'We just got on with our lives'?

That, for me, is the importance of the essays in this volume, for they focus on pastimes, events and icons that were very much part of the lives that people 'got on with' in the 1950s. Disneyland, pulp magazines, dime fiction, hairstyles, science fiction films, food, comic books, television situation comedies, clothing: these were the topics of daily conversation. The 'cultural' became the 'political', not through any grand affirmation of support for a particular policy or rally behind this or that candidate but through the everyday formation of values and practices. A trip to Disney's showcase in California brought 'freedom' and 'nation' to far more people than any town-hall meeting ever could. The popular journal, the feature film and the family den were sites of gendered constructions of power far more complex than a simple division between aggressive masculinity and passive femininity. Food, always a potent religious and social marker, became a vehicle for the coexistence of 'traditional' practice and 'modern' Americanism. To borrow from Benedict Anderson,[4] these were the sites of activity that generated 'imagined communities'.

There is no reason why this framework could not be applied to any period of US history, but there is a particular reason why it is essential to apply it to the 1950s, a reason that goes beyond the expansion of the 'cultural' from the local to the national through technology and the development of 'mass' activities and markets. When the Cold War was defined as a total conflict at home and abroad, every sector of society would be scrutinised for its contribution to the American effort. Thus, the individual's pursuit of a 'private' existence could not be detached from what governments and other organisations construed as 'public' responsibilities. As Emma Lambert notes cogently in her essay on Disneyland in this volume, 'The defining characteristic of the 1950s ... is [the] attempt to negotiate ... [the] definition of ideas of America and Americanness, through all spheres of life.'

There is a danger that this approach can be too sweeping in its exposition of the 'cultural'. A term like 'domestic containment' can be bandied about so often that analysis has little significance. Who was being contained? By what means? And, most significantly, to what end? For, while it is possible to draw multiple meanings from any cultural practice, the cutting edge for interpretation remains that attempts were constantly being made to mobilise or limit those practices for particular objectives.

Perhaps the most striking example of both the possibilities and pitfalls is in Alan Nadel's *Containment Culture*. Nadel states cogently that 'the American cold war is a particularly useful example of the power of large cultural narratives to unify, codify, and contain – perhaps *intimidate* is the best word – the personal narratives of its population'[5] before examining narratives ranging from John Hersey's *Hiroshima* to *Playboy* to *The Man Who Shot Liberty Valance*. Yet Nadel, for all the scope of his cultural survey, goes astray in two fundamental areas. First, he never establishes that his 'personal' American was intimidated by this output; not once does he examine the reception of and reaction to the large cultural narratives, let alone consider the personal narratives of the populace. Second, rather than establishing how the Government interacted with 'private' producers of the cultural narrative from 1945 to 1960, for example by considering the Government's linkage of foreign policy and domestic propaganda or by formal or unofficial links between 0the official and private spheres, he reduces State involvement to a bizarre (and wildly inaccurate) reading of one essay by one official, the State Department's George Kennan, as a 'sexual narrative of courtship and rivalry ... making the Russians horny'.[6]

My own contention is that we contain ourselves, in studying the relationship between politics and 'culture', with a simple resort to 'containment'. Cultural historians have borrowed the term 'containment' from studies of US foreign policy without realising that it is far from definitive and, indeed, misleading. Contrary to the prattling of mainstream US diplomatic historians about 'national security', the objective of the US Government from 1948 was not to contain Soviet Communism but to vanquish it. There could be no coexistence between freedom and tyranny. In the words of NSC 68:

'Unwillingly our free society finds itself mortally challenged by the Soviet system. No other value system is so wholly irreconcilable with ours, so implacable in its purpose to destroy ours, so capable of turning to its own uses the most dangerous and divisive trends in our own society, no other so skilfully and powerfully evokes the elements of irrationality in human nature everywhere, and no other has the support of a great and growing center of military power.'[7]

When the US Government finally accepted the existence of both the Soviet and Chinese blocs in 1956, it was not because of an endorsement of 'containment' but because efforts to liberate the peoples of Eastern Europe had failed spectacularly with the suppression of the Hungarian rising.

Examining the domestic dimension of this campaign, we can offer some structure of interpretation for disparate cultural experiences by establishing where governments and other groups tried to organise those experiences for total victory over the Soviet foe. In doing so, we move beyond the restrictive (and negative) notion of a containment of values and practice. The mission of both official agencies and their 'private' allies was not just to contain subversive practices at home, be it political dissent, sexual deviance or a threat to economic and social hierarchies, but to project a positive image of US culture that exalted both 'old-fashioned' and 'modern' cultural constructions. Disneyland would have both a Frontierland and Tomorrowland; classical music would take on the American forms of Gershwin and Copland but would live with jazz and even Presley; the US would make its mark at European festivals with Abstract Expressionism.

One of the most striking examples of both the positive and negative aspects of a projection linking foreign policy and domestic culture was the sustained promotion by the Eisenhower Administration of 'Atoms for Peace'. The initiative, symbolically launched by the President's speech before the United Nations in

December 1953, was not exactly a case of getting Americans and co-operative foreigners to love the bomb, but more a shifting of their attention from nasty military issues towards the great Tomorrow promised by applications of atomic power. The 'negative' dimension of the strategy was the deliberate downplaying or suppression of information about the expected casualties of an atomic attack upon the USA. The world's press and, via them, the public might have been treated to a show of US strength at testing sites, but Eisenhower and his advisors, fearing that a worried public might demand restrictions on the development of nuclear weapons, lied about the possibilities of civil defence programmes and labelled concerns about the long-term effects of radiation as 'hysteria'. The 'positive' dimension was the multimillion-dollar campaign of ships and other transport, breakthroughs in health-care, agricultural advances, and of course generation of energy, courtesy of (as Disney portrayed it) 'Our Friend the Atom'.[8]

Thus, as Kyle Smith establishes in Chapter 7 of this volume, the 'cultural' construction of the film *The Incredible Shrinking Man* first implements the 'political' neutralisation of radiation as 'a sourcelessness, a randomness, [that] one might associate with a natural disaster'. Then it projects the positive side of atomic energy through the vision of the 'man of the future'. Where the 1953 film version of *War of the Worlds* escaped the tricky question of conflict with the enemy by closing with the invocation of God, *The Incredible Shrinking Man* asks Americans to lay their concerns before the altar of progress. Both viewpoints were essential to a US Government that was combining one nation 'under God' with homage to capitalism and technology.

We can also move beyond domestic containment, however, by challenging the simple view of an elite hegemony over that area where private activity becomes public. Even Donald Pease, in his work on culture and US imperialism, risks this simplification: while he recognises that the formation of 'a coherent national identity' worked with 'diverse constituencies whose differences could only be partially and unevenly repressed', he still concludes by referring to 'the condensation of these heterogeneous social materials into a single foregrounded entity'.[9] One striking example of the problem that results is Elaine Tyler May's influential work, *Homeward Bound: American Families in the Cold War*, a book that helped launch the term 'domestic containment.'[10] Millions of women might have fit May's near-universal image of docile housewife, but many others belonged to professional organisations, held 'real' jobs, and engaged in political activity both for and against the Government of the day.[11] Another example is the virtual absence of African-Americans from studies of the Cold War at home and abroad, apart from studies of 'left-wing' individuals like W.E.B. DuBois and Paul Robeson. A cursory survey reveals that many African-Americans worked closely with 'official' agencies. Yet, while most of them would uphold the Government's insistence upon the American system rather than the Soviet counterpart as a model for progress, they would also criticise US support for colonialism in Asia and Africa as well as segregation at home.[12]

In the essays in this book, groups that could easily be stereotyped as part of the homogeneous vision of free government and free enterprise are seen to assume positions where acceptance and opposition coexist, addressing Jackson Lears' question, 'What was the relationship between subordinate cultures and the dominant culture created by professional and managerial elites?'[13] Julie Willett's work on beauticians, for example, not only highlights the economic empowerment of women as entrepreneurs but also raises the provocative question about political positions: did African-American beauticians become an opposition force helping to orchestrate pressure for civil rights legislation and social change or, given their new stake in economic stability, could they, like some African-American preachers, small businessmen, lawyers and judges, take a 'conservative' position arguing against rapid change? Nathan Abrams' essay on Mother's Old-Fashioned Gefilte Fish raises an interesting variant. To what extent were Jewish-Americans establishing a position not just of 'assimilation' but of submission or resistance? Granted that many kosher products were promoted with techniques of the mass market and, conversely, that products from

Pepsi-Cola to Maxwell House coffee became part of the kosher diet, but what of products like Jell-O that remained forbidden? Could resistance to its consumption be marked not only as the stand against Communist subversion that Abrams identifies but, alternatively or concurrently, as a protest against the culture of consumption that had promoted Jell-O as an essential 'American' food?

Even more intriguing are those cases where individuals were asked not to act but to interpret. Will Brooker's essay on homosexuality and Batman comics is illustrative. Purges of the sexually suspect from Government employment after World War II certainly reinforced a culture where not only right-wing keepers of morality but also concerned 'liberals' could search for deviancy in products like comic books. At the same time, Brooker highlights how gay men, far from rejecting this reading, could find positive affirmation in it. The same cultural signs could thus foster or reinforce both 'mainstream' and 'alternative' interpretative communities.

Or the individual could draw multiple, even conflicting, meanings from a single cultural source. Julie Hughes' study of Anya Seton's *The Winthrop Woman* points out how the reader could find the central character, Elizabeth Fones, a 'strong' woman, countering the stereotype of passive femininity in the 1950s. Yet Elizabeth's sister is depicted as 'childish' and 'pathetic', and her rape by a cousin, John Winthrop, Jr, is unquestioned. On another level, Elizabeth's questioning of Puritan codes of thought and behaviour challenges the consensual paradigm of 1950s America, as well as women's place within it, yet this elevation as a 'free-thinking' individual also 'reinforces a concept of America ... based upon romantic and bourgeois ideologies of selfhood'.

So, in recognising the multiplicity of cultural practices, do we walk away from the notion of the State and allied institutions trying to shape a private sphere that would reinforce US efforts in the Cold War?[14] No, because it might not be necessary to limit cultural positions or meanings, if agreement could be established upon certain general conceptions. Foremost among these notions was the US defence of 'freedom'. With this mantra, the Government could issue the Truman Doctrine, the clarion call for the Cold War, to 'support free peoples who are resisting attempted subjugation', even though Greece and Turkey, the two countries that had prompted the Declaration, were far from 'free' regimes.[15] NSC-68 could treble the military budget, authorise unprecedented covert action, and sanction the support of France in Indochina all because 'freedom [was] the most contagious idea in history'.[16] Conversely, the Stockholm Peace Petition of 1950, despite millions of signatures, could be dismissed because any 'peace' supported by the Soviet Union would be at the cost of freedom; indeed, an American's position on the Petition could define his or her cultural and political well-being.[17] This was a mobilisation of culture, supported as much by millions of dollars in both overt and covert subsidies from the State as it was by the coercive power of loss of employment, liberty, and/or social position. The Congress for Cultural Freedom and its American affiliate, the American Committee for Cultural Freedom, the Free Russia Fund, Freedom House, the National Committee for a Free Europe, the Committee for Free Asia, the Friends of Russian Freedom and myriad like-minded organisations and individuals benefited from Government largesse.[18]

The problem for the Government, and thus for American society, was that even 'freedom' could be contested. There was the conundrum of defending freedom by taking the rights associated with it from thousands, if not millions, of American citizens. Such a problem would split the 'liberal' anti-Communist politico-cultural elite, curbing the activities of the American Committee for Cultural Freedom and eventually contributing to its dissolution. The struggle to establish Atoms for Peace both stemmed from and reinforced a related paradox: could the Government justify more and more powerful nuclear weapons to protect the Free World when those weapons might take millions of lives? There might be *The Incredible Shrinking Man*, with its excusing of atomic technology, but there was also *The Day the Earth Stood Still*, with its warning that East–West conflict could destroy the world. For every presidential proclamation of hope, there was a cultural projection of war.

One response to this, from the ponderings of intellectual elites as well as the rhetoric of presidents, was the positing of the American 'consensus' that would later be exalted in the histories of the 1950s. Paeans to the 'end of ideology,' while being far from a coherent explanation of history and current events, would combat the threats of both McCarthyism and dissent over policy abroad and at home.[19] Yet, as few Americans would have heard of a Daniel Bell or a Richard Hofstadter, the problem remained: could the State rely upon cultural constructions of 'freedom' for the masses, be it a Cecil B. de Mille film or the proclamation of 'People's Capitalism', which might not produce the desired reaction? We might posit that the outcome was a process of politico-cultural negotiations that encompassed all aspects of daily life. For many, that negotiation might be simply to 'get on with their lives', assured of enough money for an adequate lifestyle. Others might be content with a reaffirmation of identities that sometimes reinforced each other, sometimes rested together uneasily – to be 'American', to be 'white' (or 'black'), to be a 'worker', to be a 'family' – taking political positions only when they perceived a challenge to those identities. For some, the negotiation might be catalysed by a particular issue, such as the bomb, while for a minority the process would encompass a wide range of concerns, domestic and foreign.

The negotiation did not occur on equal terms. The government and other institutions had military, economic and judicial resources that could be used as threats and/or incentives. However, I would contend that many people and groups entered these negotiations freely whether it be through the 'everyday' practices of watching television, choosing acceptable foods and styling their hair, or through direct approaches to a 'dominant' State. The National Student Association asking for funds from the State Department (and getting them eventually from the CIA); the NAACP Executive Secretary, Walter White, pledging support for the Truman Administration rather than alternatives like Henry Wallace; Ronald Reagan testifying on behalf of the Screen Actors Guild before the House Un-American Activities Committee; thousands of citizens giving millions of dollars to the Freedom Bell and the Crusade for Freedom: all serve as reminders that the Cold War was in many ways a co-operative process.

In the end, almost all Americans paid lip service to the ideology, recited the Pledge of Allegiance strengthened with the phrase 'under God', and trusted in the superiority of their country, not because they were 'contained' but because they could agree upon these basic conceptions. Few openly challenged the invocations of 'freedom' and the contradictory manifestations of it. McCarthy would be brought down not by the clamour of the masses defending their rights, but by an administration and Senate whose power and authority he threatened once too often. Whatever the qualms about atomic weapons, token steps to limit their development would come only after the hair's breadth escape from the Cuban Missile Crisis. The vast majority would accept the despatch of advisors, then bombers, then troops to Vietnam – the protests would come much, much later.[20]

So, even as we record some of the images and meanings of the 1950s and challenge the simple notion of 'containment', let us not settle for that. People might have fought at home ongoing, often surreptitious battles over sexuality, 'conformity' and economic and social positions, but most, getting on with their lives, were content to wear the mantle of being 'American'. The outcome was that US officials could pursue an aggressive, often destructive foreign policy in the 1950s. If we pursue our notion of the 'cultural' long enough, we might just meet the enemy and find that he was us.

Notes

1. William O'Neill, *American High: The Years of Confidence, 1945–1960* (New York, Free Press, 1986).
2. John Patrick Diggins, *The Proud Decades: America in War and Peace, 1941–1960* (New York, Norton, 1988).
3. I.F. Stone, *The Haunted Fifties* (London, Merlin Press, 1964).
4. Benedict Anderson, *Imagined Communities* (London, Verso, 1991).
5. Alan Nadel, *Containment Culture: American Narratives, Postmodernism, and the Atomic Age* (Durham, North Carolina, Duke University Press, 1995), p. 4.
6. Ibid. pp. 5 and 15.
7. State Department/Department of Defense Report (7 April 1950), US Declassified Document Reference System, Retrospective 71D.

8. See Scott Lucas, *Freedom's War: The US Crusade Against the Soviet Union, 1945–1956* (Manchester, Manchester University Press, 1999), Chapter 10.
9. Donald Pease, 'Hiroshima, the Vietnam Veterans War Memorial, and the Gulf War: Post War: Post-National Spectacles', in Amy Kaplan and Donald Pease, *Cultures of United States Imperialism* (Durham, USA, Duke University Press, 1993), pp. 557–8.
10. Elaine Tyler May, *Homeward Bound: American Families in the Cold War Era* (New York, Basic Books, 1988). The portrayal is even more striking in May's later survey for 'The Young Oxford History of Women in the United States'. Despite her modification that 'all [women] took advantage of new opportunities and pushed against the constraints that remained. They were not watching from the sidelines; they were on the march,' her portrayal of 'public women' is limited to one chapter, focusing on the civil rights movement and a few Great Women fighting 'liberal' causes. She then adds the wildly inaccurate statement, 'Most of the active women's organizations in the postwar years were apolitical' since they 'did little to challenge the system'. The possibility that women who voluntarily and actively supported Government domestic and foreign policy might be 'political' does not seem to arise. [Elaine Tyler May, *Pushing the Limits: American Women, 1940–1961* (Oxford, Oxford University Press, 1994), pp. 13 and 129.]
11. See, for example, Helen Laville, 'The Committee of Correspondence: The CIA and the Funding of Women's Groups, 1952–1967', *Intelligence and National Security* (January 1997), pp. 104–21; Helen Laville, 'A Women's Place is in the Cold War: American Woman's Organisations in International Relations, 1945–1965,' Ph.D. thesis, University of Nottingham, (May 1998); Joanne Meyerowitz (ed.), *Not June Cleaver* (Philadelphia, Temple University Press, 1994); and Susan Lynn, *Progressive Women in Conservative Times: Radical Justice, Peace, and Feminism, 1945–1960s* (New Brunswick, Rutgers University Press, 1992).
12. See Helen Laville and Scott Lucas, 'Edith Sampson, the NAACP, and African American Identity', *Diplomatic History* (Fall 1996), pp. 565–90; and Brenda Gayle Plummer, *Rising Wind: Black Americans and U.S. Foreign Policy, 1935–1960* (Chapel Hill, USA, University of North Caroline Press, 1996).
13. Jackson Lears, 'A Matter of Taste', in Lary May (ed.), *Recasting America: Culture and Politics in the Age of Cold War* (Chicago,

University of Chicago Press, 1989), p. 54. Interestingly, Lears never really answers his question, although he closes with a curious reference to the 1950s: 'men and women who were haunted by a fear of cultural asphyxiation, restless for stylistic novelty, and unaware that the task of resuscitation involved more than a breath of fresh air from Camelot'.

14. See the discussion of cultural history and 'private' experience in Richard Wightman Fox and T.J. Jackson Lears, 'Introduction', in *The Power of Culture: Critical Essays in American History* (Chicago, University of Chicago Press, 1993).
15. Harry Truman, *Memoirs* (Garden City, New York, Doubleday, 1956), p. 105.
16. State Department/Department of Defense Report (7 April 1950), US Declassified Document Reference System, Retrospective 71D.
17. State Department Press Release 743 (12 July 1950), US National Archives, Lot 64 D 563, Records of the Policy Planning Staff, 1947–53, Subject Files, Box 8, Communism 1947–51. See also the CIA assessment in CIA 5–50 (17 May 1950), Minutes of Meetings of the National Security Council with Special Advisory Reports, Reel 1.
18. Lucas, *Freedom's War*, Chapters 7–8.
19. Notable examples are Daniel Bell, *The End of Ideology: On the Exhaustion of Political Ideas in the Fifties* (Glencoe, USA, Free Press, 1960); and Richard Hofstadter, *The American Political Tradition: and the Men Who Made It* (New York, Vintage Books, 1954). See also Peter Novick, *That Noble Dream: The 'Objectivity Question' and the American Historical Profession* (Cambridge, Cambridge University Press, 1988).
20. Nor do I accept, despite my high regard for his critique of US foreign policy, the argument of Noam Chomsky that the 'people' did this because they were shut off from knowledge. Yes, the executive lied to them; yes, information was withheld, classified and distorted. Still, they could have picked up many threads for dissent: the obvious persecution of 'fellow travellers' for their beliefs, the obvious cost, which no deception could entirely obscure, of atomic war, the reports of religious repression, financial corruption, and military disorder in South Vietnam. People chose to support their government or, in most cases, simply did nothing. See James Peck (ed.), *The Chomsky Reader* (London, Serpent's Tale, 1988).